Minds without Meanings

Minds without Meanings

An Essay on the Content of Concepts

Jerry A. Fodor and Zenon W. Pylyshyn

The MIT Press
Cambridge, Massachusetts
London, England

MIT Press books may be purchased at special quantity discounts for business or sales promotional use. For information, please email special_sales@mitpress.mit.edu.

This book was set in Stone by the MIT Press. Printed and bound in the United States of America.

Library of Congress Cataloging-in-Publication Data

Fodor, Jerry A.
Minds without meanings : an essay on the content of concepts / Jerry A. Fodor and Zenon W. Pylyshyn.
  pages   cm
Includes bibliographical references and index.
ISBN 978-0-262-02790-8 (hardcover : alk. paper)
1. Concepts. 2. Reference (Philosophy). 3. Representation (Philosophy). I. Title.
BD181.F63   2014
121'.4—dc23
2014003811

10 9 8 7 6 5 4 3 2 1

Contents

Acronyms

ANN	Artificial neural net
BCS	Basic cognitive science
CTM	The computational theory of mind
DCT	The dual code theory (of mental representation)
EP	Empiricist principle
GW	George Washington (example)
IRS	Inferential role semantics
ITM	Inferential role theory of mind
LL	Leibniz's law
LOT	Language of thought
MOT	Multiple object tracking (experimental method)
OFP	Our first president
P&C	Prinz and Clark 2004
PA	Propositional attitude
PC	Perceptual circle
PLA	Private language argument
PRS	Purely referential semantics
RTM	Representational Theory of Mind
SI	Substitution of Identicals

1 Working Assumptions

Most of this book is a defense and elaboration of a galaxy of related theses that, as far as we can tell, no one but us believes. There are various ways to formulate these theses: that tokens of beliefs, desires, and the like are tokens of relations between minds and mental representations; that mental representations are "discursive" (which is to say, language-like); that reference is the only semantic property of mental or linguistic representations;[1] that there are no such things as word meanings or conceptual contents; that there are no such things as senses; and so on. This list is not exhaustive; we'll add to it as we go along. And we'll argue that these claims, if true, have profound implications for cognitive science, linguistics, psychology, the philosophy of language, and the philosophy of mind—all of which are, according to us, long overdue for massive revisions. We'll sketch accounts of mental representations and processes that embody such revisions and are, we think, compatible with a variety of empirical data.

We don't, however, propose to start from first principles. To the contrary, we will make a variety of quite substantive assumptions, which, though they are by no means universally endorsed in the cognitive science community, are at least less scandalous than the ones that we primarily propose to defend. We start by enumerating several of these. In the chapters to follow, we will add more and consider some of their implications.

First Assumption: Belief-Desire Psychology

To begin with, we take it that behaviorism is false root and branch; in the paradigm cases, behavior is the effect of mental causes, and the paradigm of explanation in cognitive psychology is the attribution of a creature's actions to its beliefs, intentions, desires, and its other "propositional attitudes," which are themselves typically the effects of interactions among its propositional attitudes and its innate endowments and with such of its mental processes as perceiving, remembering, and thinking. Likewise, though we assume that the mechanisms by which mental causation is implemented are in all likelihood neural, we don't at all suppose that psychological explanations can be reduced to, or replaced by, explanations in brain science—no more than we suppose that geological explanations can be reduced to, or replaced by, explanations in quantum mechanics. Confusions of ontological issues about *what mental phenomena are* with epistemological issues about *how mental phenomena are to be explained* have plagued interdisciplinary discussions of how—or whether— psychology is to be "grounded" in brain science. Current fashion prefers "central state" reductionism to the behaviorist kind, but we think, and will assume, that the prospects for both are equally dim, and for much the same reasons. "Naïve realism" is the default assumption in the psychology of cognition, just as it is everywhere else in science. Otherwise, why does it so often happen that the predictions the theories endorse turn out to be true?

The paradigm of belief-desire explanation, to which we will advert from time to time, is what Aristotle called a "practical syllogism."

Practical Syllogism

- A wants it to be the case that P.
- A believes that not-P unless Q.
- A acts so as to bring it about that Q.

We take it that explanations that invoke practical syllogisms are typically causal (beliefs and desires *cause* actions). But we think it was a mistake for Aristotle to hold that the "conclusion" of a practical syllogism is itself an action. For one thing, what syllogisms are supposed to preserve is *truth*, and actions are neither true nor false. Also, intentions to perform actions are often thwarted by facts that the agent failed to include in his reasoning (you try to scratch your nose, but somebody stops you).

Readers who wish to think such objections are mere quibbles are, however, entirely free to do so; we too think that the main point of Aristotle's story is perfectly sound: typical explanations of creatures' behaviors take them to be the effects of mental causes, and so shall we. Also, we take for granted that the question of *which* of a creature's behaviors are correctly explained by reference to its beliefs and desires is fully empirical, as is the question of which of a creature's behaviors constitute its actions. Such issues can't be settled from the armchair, much philosophy to the contrary notwithstanding. As usual, in empirical inquiry, data count, as do considerations of simplicity, plausibility, and the availability of alternative explanations.

Second Assumption: Naturalism

Mental states and processes are part of the physical world. That means, at a minimum, that the processes that cognitive science postulates must be ones that can be carried out by actual physical mechanisms, and the states that it postulates are ones that physical objects can be in. It has sometimes been suggested that naturalism, so construed, is vacuous since which states and processes count as "physical" keeps changing as physics advances. (See, e.g., Chomsky 2003.) But we don't think this objection is sustainable. What matters, from the naturalist's point of view, is not that *physics* is basic science, but only that *some science or other* is basic, and that its explanatory apparatus contains no irreducibly mentalistic vocabulary. As things stand, of course, it appears that some science more or less continuous with our current physics is overwhelmingly the most plausible candidate: the best bet is that everything that enters into causal processes, and every causal process that anything enters into, will have a true description in the vocabulary of physics, but not in, as it might be, the vocabulary of geology or meteorology or botany, and least of all in the vocabulary of psychology. Naturalism per se cares that there be a science in which all the others are rooted, and that its explanatory apparatus contains nothing mentalistic. But for our present purposes, it doesn't matter which science that is.

Like Chomsky, Hilary Putnam (2012) rejects the naturalist program in psychology, but for a reason different from Chomsky's, namely that "as a rule, naturalism is not defined" (110). In consequence, he accepts the theses that intentional idioms are "baseless" and that a science that requires them is "empty" (14). Putnam is certainly right that no one has defined 'naturalism', 'believes that', 'means that', or, indeed, any of the key methodological or theoretical terms that intentional explanations routinely employ (nobody has defined 'table' or 'chair' either, for that matter). But we wonder why Putnam thinks that shows that the intentional idiom is baseless, or anything else of much methodological interest. In fact, the theoretical vocabulary of the empirical sciences, as well as the vocabulary in terms of which methodological constraints on empirical science are formulated, is hardly *ever* defined (nor, we expect, will it ever be). *The notion of definition plays no significant role in either science or the philosophy of science, as Putnam himself has often and illuminatingly insisted.* No botanist has defined 'tree', nor has chemistry defined 'water'. ('Water is H_2O' doesn't *define* 'water'; it says *what water is*, what makes a thing water.) Likewise, empirical science often adverts to such notoriously undefined notions as 'observation', 'confirmation', 'data', 'evidence', and, for that matter, 'empirical' and 'theory'. That is not a reason to suppose that empirical theories are ipso facto empty. Even sophisticated people used to say that science consists solely of "observations and definitions." But that was a long while ago, and sophisticated people don't say that any more. Putnam himself doesn't say it, except *when he is talking about intentional science.* That does strike us as arbitrary.

Still, there are plausible grounds for arguing that naturalism rules out the kind of cognitive psychology that this book has in mind: one that takes believing, intending, and the like to be content-bearing states that are bona fide causes of behavior. Propositional attitudes are relations that minds bear to propositions; as such, they are abstract objects (as are concepts, numbers, properties, and the like). And abstract objects can't be either causes or effects. The number three can't make anything happen, nor can it be an effect of something's having happened (though, of course, a state of affairs that instantiates threeness—for example, there being three bananas on the shelf—can perfectly well be a cause of John's looking for the bananas there, or an effect of his having put the bananas there). Likewise the proposition that it is raining can't cause John to bring his umbrella; it can't even cause John to believe that it's raining.

But then, if propositions can't be causes or effects, and if propositional attitudes are relations that creatures bear to propositions, mustn't propositional attitudes themselves be likewise causally inert? After all, the difference between propositional attitudes is, often enough, just a difference between the propositions that they are attitudes toward: the difference between the propositions *Venus is red* and *Mars is red* is, quite plausibly, all that distinguishes John's believing that Venus is red from his believing that Mars is red. In short, our kind of cognitive science wants propositional attitudes to be causes of behavior, but naturalism wants propositions not to be causes of *anything*; so perhaps we can't have what we want. It wouldn't be the first time.

This is a metaphysical minefield and has been at least since Plato, and it is one in which we don't intend to wander. We will simply take for granted that abstracta are without causal powers; only "things-in-the-world" (including, in particular, individual states and events) can have causes or effects. The question is how to reconcile taking all that for granted with the naturalism of explanations in cognitive science.

Third Assumption: The Type–Token Distinction

It helps the exposition, here and further on, if we introduce the type–token distinction. If one writes 'this cat has no tail' three times, one has written three *tokens* of the same sentence *type*. Likewise if one utters 'this cat has no tail' three times. Propositions, by contrast, are *types* of which there may (or may not) be tokens either in language or (according to the kind of cognitive science we endorse) in thought. Proposition types are causally inert; but the tokens that express them—including chalk marks on blackboards, ink marks on paper, utterances of sentences, neural events, and so forth—are bona fide physical objects. The Representational Theory of Mind (RTM) proposes to extend this sort of analysis to thoughts, beliefs, and other contentful mental states and events that play a role in the causation of cognitive phenomena: mental causes that express propositions (or whatever units of content propositional attitude explanations may require) are, by stipulation, 'mental representations'. It is convenient to suppose that mental representations are neural entities of some sort, but a naturalist doesn't have to assume that if he doesn't want to. We are officially neutral; all we insist on is that, whatever else they are or aren't, mental representations are the sorts of things whose ultimate parts basic science talks about. There may be a better way out of the puzzle about how mental contents can have causal roles, but we don't know of any.

Fourth Assumption: Psychological Reality

It is sometimes suggested, both by philosophers of language and by linguists (Jackson 1977; Soames 2010; Devitt 2006) that accurate prediction of the intuitions (modal, grammatical, or both) of informants is the most that can reasonably be required in some of the cognitive sciences, in particular in linguistics. We assume, on the contrary, that intuitions are of interest in the cognitive sciences (or any other sciences) only insofar as they are ontologically reliable. And typically they are ontologically reliable only when they are effects of mental processes of the sort that the cognitive sciences study. If there aren't such processes, or if informants' intuitions about them are unreliable, who cares what informants intuit?

Fifth Assumption: Compositionality of Propositions

The propositions that are the objects of propositional attitudes (intuitively, the things that go in the blanks in such formulas as 'John believes that …'; 'John remembers that …'; 'John hopes that …'; etc.) have semantic contents; indeed, they have their semantic contents *essentially*, since propositions that differ in contents are ipso facto different propositions. The semantic content of a proposition is the joint product of (what philosophers call) its "logical syntax" together with its inventory of constituent concepts. Suppose the question arises whether the propositions *John is an unmarried man* and *John is a bachelor* are identical (and hence whether believing that John is a bachelor is the same mental state as believing that John is an unmarried man). By stipulation, it is if and only if UNMARRIED MAN and BACHELOR are the same concepts.[2]

In short, we assume that propositions are structured objects of which concepts are the constituents, much as English sentences are structured objects of which words (or, if you prefer, morphemes) are the constituents. Some *concepts* are also syntactically structured (e.g., the concept GRAY SKY) and some (including, perhaps, the concepts GRAY and SKY) are "primitive." Analogies between propositions and sentences and between words and concepts aren't, of course, accidental; propositions are what (declarative) sentences *express*, and (excepting idioms, metaphors, and the like), *which* proposition a sentence expresses is determined by its syntax and its inventory of constituents. So the sentence 'John loves Mary' expresses a different proposition than the sentence 'Mary loves John' or the sentence 'John loves Sally'. Likewise, the *thought* that *John loves Mary* expresses a different proposition than either the thought that *Mary loves John* or the thought that *John loves Sally*. That thoughts and sentences match up so nicely is part of why you can sometimes say what you think and vice versa.

Sixth Assumption: Compositionality of Mental Representations

If one believes that propositions are compositional, it is practically inevitable that one believes that mental representations are too. The proposition *John loves Mary* is true in virtue of John's loving Mary. That's because it contains appropriately arranged constituents that refer to (the individuals)[3] John and Mary, and to (the relation) of loving. Likewise, the *mental representation* JOHN LOVES MARY expresses the proposition *John loves Mary* (and is expressed, in English, by the sentence 'John loves Mary'). That's because it contains appropriately arranged constituents that are mental representations of John and Mary, and of loving. The compositionality of mental representations (and of sentences) thus mirrors the compositionality of the propositions they express. This arrangement does lots of useful work. For example, it explains why what one thinks when one thinks about John's loving Mary is, inter alia, something about John, Mary, and loving.[4]

Seventh Assumption: The Representational Theory of Mind (RTM)

So far, then:

• Cognitive phenomena are typically the effects of propositional attitudes.

• Relations between minds and propositions are typically mediated by relations between minds and mental representations that express the propositions. For expository purposes, we'll refer to the conjunction of these theses as "the Representational Theory of Mind" (RTM).

We do understand that for some readers RTM may be a lot to swallow even as a working hypothesis. Still, we aren't going to defend it here; suffice it that we're pretty much convinced that RTM will have to be swallowed if cognitive science is to be interpreted realistically; that is, as a causal account of how the cognitive mind works.

The idea that cognitive processes typically consist of causal chains of tokenings of mental representations isn't itself at all radical, or even particularly new. It is almost always taken for granted in both classical rationalist and classical empiricist philosophy of mind, and it is at least as old as Aristotle, Ockham, Descartes, Locke, and Hume. To be sure, our version of RTM differs in a number of ways from its classical formulations. We don't, for example, think that mental representations are images (images have a terrible time expressing propositions, which thoughts do routinely). And we aren't associationists; that is, we think that mental processes are typically causal interactions among mental representations, but not that such interactions are typically governed by the putative 'laws of association'. To the best of our knowledge, embracing RTM is the only way that a naturalist in cognitive science can manage to avoid associationism and/or behaviorism, both of which we take to be patently untenable. More on this as we go along.

Eighth Assumption: The Computational Theory of Mind (CTM)

Since mental representations are compositional, they must have constituent structure. In the sort of cognitive psychology that was typical of Empiricism, the assumption was that the structure of the mental representations of propositions was associative. (Likewise, the structure of mental representations of "complex" concepts, i.e., of all concepts that aren't primitives.) To a first approximation: mental representations of complex concepts are built from associations among mental representations of primitive concepts, and mental representations of propositions are associations among primitive or complex concepts (or both). Roughly, the mental representation that expresses the proposition *John loves Mary* consists of the associated constituents JOHN, LOVES, and MARY, as does the mental representation that expresses the proposition *Mary loves John*.

However, various considerations, some of which will be discussed later in this book, have made the inadequacy of this associationist/empiricist account of conceptual structure increasingly apparent. Rather, in the sort of cognitive science that is currently favored by empiricists, the structure of mental representations of complex concepts and of propositions is assumed to be *syntactic:* they both have constituent structures (see above). This offers the possibility of a new view of cognitive mental *processes* (in particular, of thinking): cognitive processes are *computations*, which is to say that cognitive processes are operations defined over the constituent structures of mental representations of the concepts and propositions that they apply to, which they may supplement, delete, or otherwise rearrange. Thus the suggested analogy, ubiquitous in both the popular and the scientific literature these days, between minds and computers. This transition from associative to computational accounts of cognitive processes has the look of a true scientific revolution; it has opened up the possibility of assimilating work in cognitive psychology to work in logic, computer science, and AI. In what follows, we will take for granted that some version of a computational account of cognitive processes will prove to be correct. Suffice it for now to emphasize that the unification of current accounts of mental representations with current accounts of mental processes depends on *both* the assumption that the structure of typical mental representations is syntactic (rather than associative) *and* the assumption that typical mental processes are computations. Give up either, and you lose some of the main benefits of holding onto the other.[5]

Ninth Assumption: The Priority of Thought to Language

We think that, in the course of linguistic communication, forms of speech inherit their semantic contents from the concepts and thoughts that they express, not vice versa. The reason that English speakers often utter the word 'cat' when they wish to say something about cats is that, in English, 'cat' refers to cats. We take this to be very nearly a truism.

Still, why not go the other way around? Why not say that the semantics of linguistic forms is at the bottom of the pile; it's what explains the semantics of propositional attitudes, thoughts, and the like? Call that the "language first" view and ours the "thought first" view. We say, to put it roughly, that forms of speech inherit their semantic properties from those of the thoughts they are used to express. The opposition says, to put it equally roughly, that thoughts inherit their semantic properties from the forms of words that are used to express them. In effect, the options are: "you can think about cats because you speak a language in which you can talk about them" or "you can talk about cats because you have thoughts about cats that your language is able to express." Which, if either, of these views is right?

There is, in both philosophy and psychology, an enormous literature according to which mental states have semantic content only because they are the states of the minds of language-using creatures. But we don't believe a word of that; usually either radical behaviorism or radical empiricism (or both) lurk in the background, and the credentials of those views have long expired. This is yet another of those cases where bad philosophy has blunted perfectly reasonable commonsense intuitions.

There are very plausible reasons for holding that learning and using "natural" languages (English, Bantu, Russian, whatever) itself presupposes complex cognitive capacities; certainly neither philosophy nor cognitive science has thus far offered serious grounds for doubting that it does. For example, a tradition in the philosophy of mind claims that John's saying X because he intended to say X is *not* an instance of a mental event with a certain content *causing* a behavior that expresses that content. Rather, it's a matter of the content of John's behavioral dispositions being manifested in his behavior (cf. 'John wanted a banana to eat so he took one off the shelf'). But that simply can't be right: John's being disposed to do such and such isn't a sufficient condition for his doing it; and it's tautological that whatever explains John's doing X *must* have been a sufficient condition for his having done it. That a vase is fragile *can't* explain why it broke, though *John's dropping* the fragile vase perhaps can.

Wittgenstein and Ryle seem to have grasped this point. Accordingly, they suggested that what explains John's doing such and such is not, after all, his disposition to do it; it's his disposition to do it *in certain circumstances*, one or another of which obtained when John *X*ed. It is then incumbent upon the dispositional explanation of John's behavior to provide an account of the conditions under which the disposition in question will be behaviorally manifested, but that is not generally possible. As Chomsky famously pointed out (Chomsky 1959), holding a gun to John's head and saying, as it might be, "Do *X* or I'll shoot" will quite probably get John to do *X*; but so too will John's just feeling like *X*-ing and seeing no reason why he shouldn't. So too with innumerably many other states of affairs that may activate John's disposition. The long and short of it is that either dispositional explanations of behavior don't explain the behavior, or the dispositions that do aren't finitely specifiable. Dilemma.

Here's another standard argument against "language before thought": Language learning—including, in particular, first-language learning—takes a lot of thinking on the part of the learner. So, if you have to be able to talk before you are able to think, it follows that you can't learn a first language. This seems to be an embarrassment since, in point of fact, many children do so. Wittgenstein (1958) and Skinner (1957/1992) both held that first-language acquisition is somehow the effect of "training" ("socially mediated reinforcement," or the like). But that can't be right either, since it turns out that children generally neither need nor get much language training in the course of learning a first language. Still more to the point, there is (as far as we know) no serious suggestion anywhere in either psychology or philosophy as to how, in the case of first-language acquisition, training might work its putative effects. (Skinner assumed that learning theory would provide the required explanation, but that proved to be a dead end. Wittgenstein dispensed altogether with theories of learning, offering instead the suggestion that what happens in first-language acquisition is that the child learns how to play certain "language games" [presumably along the lines of Jane-says-'slab'; Tarzan-brings-slab]. But no details are provided.)

In short: acquiring a first language is, prima facie, a very complex cognitive achievement; so far, neither pigeons nor computers are able to do it; nor has cognitive science been able, so far, to explain it. So it's hard to imagine how first-language learning could proceed in a creature that lacks quite a lot of prior conceptual sophistication. Here, in case they are needed, are some further reasons for holding that, in the order of explanation as in the order of cognitive ontogenesis, thought comes first and language follows after:

• Thought-first avoids having to claim, from the armchair, that neither animals nor preverbal infants can think. But whether they can think is surely an empirical issue, and, to our knowledge, there is no evidence that they can't. The thesis that (excepting, perhaps, occasional reflexes) newborns are cognitively inert has become increasingly unattractive since the collapse of the Piagetian program in developmental cognitive psychology.

• Thought-first may explain the intuition that we can't *always* say what we think (cf. the notorious tribulations of lawyers, logicians, and poets).

• Thought-first may explain the intuition that we can almost always think what we say (cf.: 'I can't tell what I think until I hear myself say it', which is either just a joke or patently false).

• Thought-first may explain why we can communicate much of what we think to people who speak our language.

• Thought-first may explain why (with translation) we can communicate much of what we think, even to people who *don't* speak our language.

• Thought-first may explain why, even if the Whorf hypothesis (according to which one's perceptual and cognitive processes are profoundly affected by which language one speaks) turns out not to be true, much of the evidence suggests that the effects of one's language on one's thought, perception, cognitive style, and the like are pretty marginal. (For discussion, see Li, Abarnell, Gleitman, and Papafragou 2011.)

Of course, none of that is even close to conclusive. But we think it's sufficiently persuasive to warrant taking the priority of thought to language as a working hypothesis and seeing where it leads; notoriously, the way to prove a pudding is to eat it and see what happens.

Summary: Basic Cognitive Science (BCS)

So far, we've supposed that beliefs and intentions are typical causes of behavior; hence that belief-desire causal explanation in cognitive psychology is OK (at least in principle); and that you can't learn or speak a language, including a first language, unless you can already think. The conjunction of these constitutes what we will call "basic cognitive science" (BCS), which we embrace wholeheartedly, and which we recommend that you embrace wholeheartedly too. Readers who dislike BCS and wish to deny any (or all) of our working assumptions are in debt for arguments against them and for at least a sketch of plausible alternatives. BCS has now been around, in some version or other, at least since the middle of the twentieth century, but thus far there have been no serious attempts at either refuting or replacing it.

We don't wish to suggest, even for a minute, that if you accept BCS all your worries about cognition will thereupon disappear. Quite the contrary. For example, we remarked that it is characteristic of cognitive science to offer theories in which tokens of propositional attitudes figure as causes and effects; and that, by definition, propositional attitudes have semantic contents. So cognitive science (very much including BCS) raises two questions that more familiar sciences do not, and to which nobody has yet got a satisfactory answer: Just what *is* semantic content, and just what role should it play in a cognitive science that is, by assumption, naturalistic? Both of these questions are very hard, and we think that the ways of answering them that cognitive science has thus far proposed are wildly unsatisfactory. The rest of this book hopes, in the words of our epigraph, to "start all over again."

We end this chapter on the note we just sounded: very likely, many readers will not be inclined to grant some (or perhaps any) of our working hypotheses. So be it. But not liking a hypothesis is not, in and of itself, grounds for rejecting it; one has the obligations of refuting it and offering serious alternatives. To our knowledge, neither of these burdens has been taken up by the (many) cognitive scientists who disapprove of BCS; and we doubt that either is likely to be in any future that we are now able to foresee. And any old theory is better than none; "out of nothing, nothing comes."

2 Concepts Misconstrued

Many of the working assumptions we endorsed in chapter 1 imply, directly or otherwise, constraints on theories of concepts and on theories of the mental representations that express concepts. For example, we've assumed that mental representations expressing concepts are the constituents of mental representations expressing the objects of propositional attitudes; we've assumed that concepts are productive, and that some of them (the "complex" concepts) have internal syntactic structure but others (the "primitive" concepts) do not; we've assumed the psychological reality and causal involvement of mental representations of concepts and their internal structures; we've assumed that typical cognitive processes are sensitive to the conceptual inventories and structures of mental representations that they apply to; and so forth. That is, to be sure, a considerable inventory of assumptions to impose on what purports to be an empirical theory of the cognitive mind. But so be it. "Qualia," "raw feels," and such aside, everything in the mind that has content at all is either a primitive concept or a construction out of primitive concepts. This isn't to endorse any version of the "empiricist principle" that there is nothing in the mind that is not first in sensation; we are, so far, uncommitted as to what primitive concepts there are or what structures they can enter into. For all we've said so far, the primitive concepts might include ELEPHANT or CARBURETOR.

It shouldn't be surprising that so much of the cognitive science literature (and of this book) is devoted to the nature of concepts, conceptual structures, and conceptual content. Once a psychologist has made up his mind about concepts, much of the rest of what he says about cognition is a forced option. But it is one thing to propose constraints on theories of concepts; it's quite another to propose an empirically adequate theory that satisfies the constraints. We now turn to our attempt to do so. That will come in three parts. In this chapter, we will offer a critical (and frequently tendentious) review of the main theories of concepts that are currently on offer in the cognitive science literature. Chapter 3 will explain why we think that they are, without exception, irredeemably wrong-headed: they all presuppose a more or less "Fregean" account of conceptual content; and, as Frege agreed, his sort of semantics would appear to rule out even the possibility of an empirical psychology of cognition.

Concepts as Mental Images

The root idea is that thinking about a martini is having a mental image of a martini, and a mental image of a martini is much like a photograph of a martini except that it is "in the head" rather than on the mantelpiece. So, if you believe, as many psychologists still do, that people have generally reliable access to what goes on in their minds ("How could I doubt my belief that I now have a mental image of a martini? Could my mind's eye be lying to my mind's mind?"), you may well wish to say that when you entertain a concept, your mind makes a picture of whatever it is a concept of.

This isn't to say that introspective plausibility is the only reason for taking image theories of concepts seriously, although at the end of the day it continues to be a main motivation, even when not explicitly announced. As a result of this strong intuition, there is a huge literature purporting to show that psychophysical studies of episodes of thought reveal certain patterns consistent with a picture-like object playing a role in reasoning. From our perspective, one might ask whether this means that images constitute a form of concept. Or does it mean that concepts are not the only form of thought—that there are nonconceptual objects in the mind that play a central role in thought? A widely held belief among psychologists (e.g., Paivio 1991), as well as popular writers, is that there are two distinct forms of thought: verbal and pictorial (where "verbal" often serves as a way of referring to any symbolic system). This has been referred to as the "dual code theory" (DCT) of mental representations, to which we will return below.[1]

While early empirical support for a dual code view came from studies of learning[2] (specifically associative learning of lists and pairs of words), the more recent empirical support relies on measurements of such psychophysical properties as reaction times, interpreted as an indicator of mental properties of the cognitive process, and of the form of the representations involved. The most frequently cited of these lines of study claim to reveal that images have *spatial* properties. The claim gets its intuitive grip from experiments taken to show that operations on a mental image present a similar pattern of reaction times as would be expected if the operations were carried out on the perceived world. For example, imagine something like a dot moving over your mental image. The time it takes to traverse a certain imagined distance is found to increase linearly with the imagined distance. Similarly, the time it takes to rotate an imagined shape increases with the angle through which the imagined shape is rotated, just as it would if you rotated a picture of that shape. The same is true for many other operations one can imagine performing on an imagined object, such as judging which two specified edges of a particular paper cutout would be conjoined if the paper were folded in a certain way to make a three-dimensional shape. And perhaps most intriguing, the time it takes an observer to report seeing a small detail in an imagined "small" image takes longer than the time to report the same detail in an imagined "large" image. Many experiments show that people typically solve such problems by imagining the spatially displayed objects (laid out in the space before them) and then carrying out imagined actions on them within this allocentric frame of reference.[3] Accordingly, these (and perhaps hundreds of similar examples) are taken to entail the presence in the mind of something very much like a rigid picture-like object, which would in turn require that the image be instantiated on a surface on which features such as lines and angles, as well as properties such as relative lengths or angular size, satisfy the axioms of Euclidean geometry and the axioms of measure theory.[4]

But that is highly implausible when applied to a mental object (do mental objects *have* size, color, weight, temperature, or do they merely *represent* such properties?). Even real pictures lack the kind of properties some people assume are true of mental pictures. Nobody these days believes that mental images of red squares are red and square in any but a phenomenological (or perhaps even a metaphorical) sense. And conversely, the instantiation of a mental image, presumably in the brain, has properties that the depicted scene does not have—such as temperature, blood flow, and electrical discharge.

Introspective plausibility has led to other unlikely claims about mental images. For example, a widely held view among both psychologists and writers in the popular press is that there are two distinct kinds of thought: verbal (i.e., language-like) and pictorial. This is the dual code theory of mental representation (DCT). The impact that DCT has had on psychology cannot be underestimated. In the 1960s and 1970s, much of cognitive psychology was concerned with discovering the parameters that affect leaning and recall. Of these, "frequency of occurrence" was said to be the most important. DCT opened the door to the suggestion that it is less the exogenous frequency than the endogenous format of a mental representation that is the primary determinant of recall (although "format" in this context was limited to serial-verbal or sentential form, or to pictorial display form). This dual code view, initially put forward by Allan Paivio (1971), is so intuitively plausible that it is widely endorsed even now.

We think that DCT did well to emphasize the similarities between certain forms of mental representations and linguistic representations; that theme will recur throughout this book. But DCT also says that some concepts (or at least some tokens of concepts) consist of mental words in one's native language while other concepts consist of mental pictures. Although neither of these is tenable (there are neither actual words nor actual pictures in the mind), the first claim—that concepts share some important characteristics with language—will be developed as we go along. But we doubt the theory that a concept is a mental picture of things can be sustained in any nontrivial form, for a number of reasons that we will sketch below.

First Reason Why Concepts Can't Be Images: Some Concepts Apply to Things That Can't Be Pictured

Berkeley famously pointed out (in his *Essay Toward a New Theory of Vision*) that the image theory fails for "abstract" concepts. You can picture a triangle, but you can't picture triangularity per se, that is, the property that triangles have in common as such (in fact, you can't really image a triangle without imaging, as Berkeley put it, a triangle that is *either equilateral or scalene*, or *isosceles or acute*, or *obtuse or right angled*, nor without imagining a white or black or a small or large triangle, and so on). But one does have a concept that expresses the property that all triangles have in common, namely, the concept TRIANGLE. Likewise, you can picture a chair, but not the property of being a chair, which is what all chairs have in common as such, and so on. The problem, in all such cases, is that the property shared by all and only things in the extension of the concept (i.e., the things that the concept applies to) can't be pictured. In fact, you can't picture *a property* as such *at all. The best you can do is picture something that has that property.* Yet, we do think about triangles and chairs from time to time, as when we think "Some chairs are comfortable" or "Not all triangles are oblique." The right conclusion is surely the one that Berkeley drew: at least some of our concepts cannot be images. That, indeed, is what Berkeley's arguments are generally said to have shown: mental images can't be concepts of abstract objects.

But it's a mistake to think of Berkeley's point as applying *only* to concepts of abstract objects. Consider your concept JOHN. Just as the concept TRIANGLE is too abstract to resemble all triangles per se, so your concept JOHN is too abstract to resemble the individual John in all his possible appearances. A photograph of

John shows how he looks now, from this viewpoint, under this lighting, and in this context, and so on, much as an image of a triangle shows how *that* triangle looks. But the concept TRIANGLE applies to each triangle as such, and the concept JOHN applies to John as such (in other words, they apply to every possible token of triangle or of John). This shows something important: concepts don't work like images. JOHN doesn't apply to John in virtue of resembling all his possible instances any more than TRIANGLE applies to triangles in virtue of resembling all of them. Berkeley's arguments are not about how "abstract" concepts differ from "concrete" concepts; they're about how concepts differ from images. Or, to put it slightly differently, they're about how the "expressive power" of iconic symbols differs from the expressive power of discursive symbols. Considerations of their expressive power suggest that concepts (more precisely, the mental representations that express them) might be a lot like words. We'll see presently that there are many reasons for holding that concepts are a lot like words and none of them apply to the claim that concepts are a lot like pictures. That is the substance of the "language of thought" (LOT) hypothesis (Fodor 1975).

There is doubtless much of interest to say about implications for cognitive theory of differences between iconic and discursive symbol systems (for more on the issue of "visual thinking," see Pylyshyn 2003, ch. 8). The use of different forms of representations, differing perhaps in expressive power, or at least in which inferences are left as unmarked, is a special case of various trade-offs that can be made in the design of computational systems, trade-offs between the expressive power of certain forms of representation and the computational complexity of drawing inferences from them.[5]

Second Reason Why Concepts Can't Be Images: "Black Swan" Arguments

The kinds of points we've just been making are familiar from philosophy. But other considerations, less widely recognized, also tend to the conclusion that concepts can't be images (mental or otherwise). Some of them are very important when issues about the relations between conceptualization and perception are at the fore.[6]

Perception interacts with prior ("standing") beliefs. All else equal, seeing a black swan reduces one's previous epistemic commitment to the belief that all swans are white. How does this work? The image theory offers what may seem, at first glance, a tidy suggestion: believing that all swans are white consists in having a mental image that shows all swans as being white (at least all visible ones). Seeing a black swan causes the formation of a mental image of a black swan. If the two images match, you decrease your epistemic commitment to the belief that all swans are white (and/or decrease your epistemic commitment to the belief that this swan is black). (We return to the problem of drawing inferences about black swans later in this book.)

But that account could not be right. To the contrary, black swan arguments show that the mental representations corresponding to perceptions and beliefs must both have a kind of semantics that images do not have. Draw a picture that shows a black swan. Now draw a picture that shows all swans are white.[7] Now draw a picture that shows these two pictures to be incompatible. It can't be done; compatibility isn't a kind of relation that pictures can express. This is one of the respects in which the expressive capacity of "discursive" representation much exceeds that of "iconic" representation, as does the expressive power of thought. Once again, it appears that cognition can't be much like photography.

Third Reason Why Concepts Can't Be Images: Constituent Structure

Concepts can have constituents, but images only have parts. For example, the complex concept MARY AND HER BROTHERS, which refers to Mary and her brothers, has a constituent that refers to Mary and a constituent that refers to her brothers. A crucial problem (the problem of compositionality) is: How do the referents of complex concepts derive from the referents of their less complex constituents? What makes this problem crucial is that solving it appears to be the only way to explain why concepts are productive (*vide*: MARY'S BROTHER; MARY'S BROTHER'S BROTHER; MARY'S BROTHER'S BROTHERS; etc.). And the productivity of concepts is needed to explain why there are so many of them that one is able to have and so many thoughts that one is able to think. A precisely analogous situation arises with respect to the phrases and sentences of natural languages: It's because 'Mary's brother' and 'Mary's brother's brothers' are among their constituents that 'Mary's brother is tall' and 'Mary's brother's brothers are tall' are both sentences.

Neither the productivity of thoughts nor the nature of the productivity of sentences is fully understood. But enough seems clear to add to our list of ways that concepts are different from images.

Consider, to begin with, the productivity of pictures. Presumably there are indefinitely many of those, just as there are indefinitely many concepts, indefinitely many thoughts, and indefinitely many sentences. That's because pictures have parts, and (arguably) the result of putting the parts of a picture together is also a picture, and it too has parts. A picture of Mary and her brother can be analyzed into parts, some of which are pictures of Mary (or parts of Mary) and some of which are pictures of Mary's brother (or parts of him). But it is also perfectly possible to make a picture that shows Mary's left arm and her brother's nose. (Think of all the ways in which you could carve up a picture of Mary and her brother into a jigsaw puzzle.) That's why you often can't put the pieces of a picture back together unless you already know (or can guess) what it is a picture of.

The difference between something's having constituents (as thoughts and sentences do) and its only having parts (as pictures do) now becomes apparent: if a symbol has parts that are constituents, there are rules (in effect, syntactic rules) for combining the parts in a way that is guaranteed to produce a more complex symbol that is itself a possible constituent; and you can follow such rules even if you don't already know what that complex constituent means. If, for example, the grammar of English is in force, the set of words 'of friend a John's' can be put together in only one way that makes a well-formed phrase. That, fundamentally, is why you can use English to communicate news. Sam says to Bill, "A friend of John's died"; and if Bill knows English, he can figure out that Sam has told him that a friend of John's died, which may well be news to Bill. What a lovely invention! You just can't do that sort of thing with pictures.

Pictures have parts but not constituents; so if concepts are pictures, they too must have parts but not constituents. Since, however, concepts have both, it follows that concepts aren't pictures.

One more point along these lines and we can then go on to yet other reasons why concepts can't be pictures. It's important, in thinking about whether pictures have constituents, to keep in mind not just the distinction between constituents and parts, but also the distinction between the parts of a picture and the parts of what it pictures. Arguably at least, things-in-the-world have parts that may, or may not, be among their constituents. (Maybe the constituents of an automobile are its "functional" parts: if so, the drive chain of a car is among its constituents, but an arbitrary piece of the front seat cover probably isn't.) This sort of distinction has implications for psychology: for example, "memory-images," when they fragment, tend to respect the constituent structure of what they are memories of, not just arbitrary collections of its parts (Pylyshyn 1973). Thus, you may "lose" part of a memory-image of John and Mary, but it's likely to be a part that represents John or a part that represents Mary (rather than, say, a part that represents a combination of John's nose and Mary's toes). But this consideration doesn't tend to show that pictures of John and Mary have constituents; at most it shows that John and Mary do. So the question remains whether mental images (as opposed to the things that mental images represent) have constituents or only parts; if, as we're suggesting, they have only the latter, then mental images are, once again, very poor candidates for being concepts.

Fourth Reason Why Concepts Can't Be Images: Leibniz's Law Arguments

Real images (pictures, drawings) share some, but not all, of their properties with the things they are images of (since they derive from geometrical/optical projections of the objects they depict).[8] But it's hard to see how mental images could do so unless one assumes that they are identified with parts of the brain, such as the surface of the visual cortex. If so, then pieces of the cortex can have (at least some of) the properties that mental images do. For example, some psychologists have managed to persuade themselves that mental images of big things (i.e., mental images of things that show them as being big) correspond to big pieces of the cortex, mental images of little things correspond to little pieces of the cortex, and so on (see, e.g., Kosslyn 1975, 1994). Even so, there are lots of kinds of cases where it's just not possible to believe that anything "in the head," be it cortex or otherwise, has the same properties that corresponding mental images seem to introspection to have. Suppose, for example, that one's mental images are indeed displayed on the surface of one's visual cortex. Still, it's not credible that the pieces of the cortex on which the images are displayed have many of the other properties that the image does. Surely it isn't true that red mental images (that's to say, mental images of red) correspond to red pieces of the cortex; the cortex is (more or less) gray. Similarly, a vertical (or horizontal) elongated figure may not be represented in cortex as a vertical (or horizontal) elongated patch. Nor do auditory images of loud sounds correspond to loud regions of cortex. The problem, of course, arises from confounding the form with the content of images. Likewise, as we mentioned earlier, the time it takes to perform a certain operation on a mental image varies with the time that it would take to perform that operation on the thing that it is an image of. Our point is that, however subjects perform such tasks, nothing in their visual cortex moves when their mental image depicts such motion. Moreover, all the psychophysical data, as well as the phenomenology of mental imagery, suggest that if spatial operations (such as scanning or rotation) apply literally to mental images, then the images and operations must be in three dimensions. In particular, they can't be operations on the two-dimensional[9] surface of the visual cortex. (There are many other empirical reasons why mental images couldn't be displayed on the visual cortex. Some are discussed in Pylyshyn 2003a, 2007.) They include: impaired mental imagery and impaired visual perception can occur independent of one another; activity patterns in V1 are retinotopic whereas mental images are in allocentric coordinates (they do not appear to move when you move your eye or head); a mental image superimposing on a visual scene fails to scale the image according to Emmert's law (the farther away the visual background is, the larger the objects in the mental image ought to appear—as they are when an afterimage is superimposed on a perceived scene); mental images are intensional objects—unlike pictures, mental images are already interpreted and can't be reinterpreted in the way that ambiguous pictures can. (Empirical support for these and other such important differences between mental images and displays in V1 is discussed in Pylyshyn 2003, ch. 4, and Pylyshyn 2007, ch. 5.)

Leibniz's law[10] arguments seem to show that nothing that is literally 'in your head' can have the properties that mental images are said to have; and if your images aren't in your head, where could they be? We don't say these kinds of objections can't be answered; as usual, a lot depends on what you're prepared to swallow. But we do say that, if they can't be answered, then the suggestion that there are mental images, neural or otherwise, makes no clear sense.

It's likewise hard to take literally the idea that introspecting a mental image is a kind of seeing it. It's worth spending a moment on this, because it seems to attract many image theorists. Mental images can't literally be *seen* any more than they can literally be *touched*. If introspection is a kind of mental seeing in which the actual, physical visual system is engaged, then mental images must be kinds of things that can reflect patterns of light that the visual system can detect. But there isn't anything of that sort. Brains, unlike mirrors, don't reflect anything. It's very dark in your head. Moreover, there are many clear differences between how vision works and how visualizing an image works (as Sartre [1948] said, there are no surprises in your mental image—it only depicts what you want it to depict, given what you believe about how things look and behave). Unlike the perception of actual visual patterns, the apparent "perception" of a mental image lacks most of the signature properties of visual perception, such as the spontaneous perception of line drawings as three-dimensional objects, the spontaneous reversal of ambiguous figures, and most visual illusions. If information is provided nonvisually (e.g., by description) so that it enables a person to create a particular image, such properties are not observed in that image (see the examples in Pylyshyn 2003a).

Other Options for Representing Concepts

Concepts as Definitions

The view of concepts as definitions is perhaps the most familiar. It says there are two aspects of a concept's content: its reference and its "meaning" (or "intension" [with an 's'], or its "sense"). The extension of a concept is the set of things that the concept applies to (according to the view we're inclined toward, it's the set of actual or possible things that the concept applies to; see chapter 3). The intension of a concept is the property in virtue of which things belong to its extension. So, for example, if the intension of the concept CAT (and hence the meaning of the word 'cat') is supposed to be 'domestic feline', then it expresses the property of being a domestic feline and all and only domestic felines belong to its extension.

That is probably more or less the semantic theory they taught you in grade school. No doubt, they did so because they believed that words express concepts and that concepts are something like definitions. That, in turn, is why your teachers kept telling you how important it is for you to "define your terms," thereby making clear exactly which concepts you have in mind when you use them. But, like so much else of what they taught you in grade school, the theory that concepts are definitions most likely isn't true. We'll presently say why it isn't, but let's start with some of its virtues.

• As we just saw, the theory that concepts are definitions seems to explicate the relation between their contents[11] and their extensions. Likewise, the theory that concepts are definitions suggests a prima facie plausible account of *having* a concept: to have a concept is to know its definition. In some cases a stronger condition is endorsed: to have a concept is to know not just its definition but also how to *apply* its definition (i.e., how to tell whether something is in the concept's extension). Philosophers of a verificationist turn of mind, in particular, often like to think of having a concept as knowing "ways of telling" (a.k.a. "criteria" for telling) whether something falls under it. The attraction of verificationism is that it seems to avoid the (crazy) skeptical thesis that there is no way of telling "for sure" what kind of thing something is. At the very least, if a concept is some sort of verification procedure, then one can tell for sure whether something is in its extension.

• Many philosophers, and more psychologists than you might suppose,[12] have thought that semantics should underwrite some notion of 'analytic' truth ("truth in virtue of meaning alone"), thereby connecting semantic issues with issues about modality. If it's true by definition that cats are felines, then there can't be a cat that isn't a feline, not even in "possible worlds" other than our own; that is, the extension of CAT contains neither any actual nor any possible cats that aren't felines. So if you think that there couldn't be such cats, you may well think that the definitional account of linguistic (and/or conceptual) content is the very semantic theory you require, since it purports to explain why there can't be. ("Linguistic semantics" and "analytic philosophy" both have a vested interest here, since both rely heavily on informants' intuitions of modality as data for their theories.)

• It is plausible, at first blush, that the definition story about conceptual content accounts for the fact that concepts compose, that is, that you can make up new concepts by putting old ones together. (By contrast, see the discussion above of the troubles that composition makes for image theories of concepts.) The putative explanation is that concepts compose because concepts are definitions and definitions compose. If you have the concepts BROWN and DOG (that is, if you know their definitions) you can compute the content (i.e., the definition) of the concept BROWN DOG; a brown dog is anything that satisfies both the definition of 'brown' and the definition of 'dog'. And if you have the concept BROWN DOG and the concept BARK, you can likewise figure out the content of the concept BROWN DOG THAT BARKS; by definition, a brown dog that barks is anything that falls under the concepts BROWN, DOG, and BARKS. And so on ad infinitum. That might answer the question of how a merely finite brain can master an indefinitely large repertoire of concepts, so it may begin to make the definition theory of conceptual content look somewhat promising.

Nonetheless, concepts aren't definitions. Here are some of the reasons why they aren't:

Most words just don't have definitions, which they surely would if the concepts they express *are* definitions. More than anything else, it's the lack of a robust supply of clear examples that has led to the recent steep decline in popularity of the definitional account of conceptual content in cognitive science.[13]

Still, there is a scattering of words/concepts that really do seem to have definitions (e.g., BACHELOR $=_{df}$ 'unmarried man'; and maybe WANT ... $=_{df}$ 'desire to have ...', etc.). These provide the standard examples in introductory linguistic semantics courses, where they have become dull with overuse. Then too, there are concepts drawn from specialist vocabularies. These are, often enough, the products of explicit agreements and stipulations. So, a yawl is a two-masted sailing vessel of which the after mast is stepped forward of the helm. Similarly, a square is a four-sided closed figure, all the sides of which are straight lines of the same length that intersect at 90 degree angles; the Jack is the card that comes between the ten and the Queen in a standard deck; and so forth.

Such definitions often do specify more or less necessary and sufficient conditions for being in corresponding extensions, and they are typically learned by explicit instruction. But they clearly don't suggest themselves as plausible exemplars for a general theory of word or concept meaning. Here are some examples drawn from a dictionary that we happen to have at hand: a 'game' is "a contest governed by a set of rules, entered into for amusement, as a test of prowess, or for money, or for other stakes." But, as Wittgenstein pointed out, skipping rope doesn't count as a game by this criterion. Nor does a discarded tin can count as 'garbage' according to our dictionary, which says that garbage is "refuse from a kitchen, etc. consisting of unwanted or unusable pieces of meat, vegetable matter, egg shells, etc." Such "definitions" are too open to determine extensions (note the "etc."), nor are they seriously intended to do so. You may have been taught in grade school that a good way to "define a term" is to look it up in a dictionary. But it bears emphasis that dictionary entries generally don't provide definitions in that sense of 'definition'. Rather, dictionary entries are typically meant to be informal guides to usage for an intended reader who already knows the language in which the defined term occurs and can thus pick up a new term from a scattering of examples (together, sometimes, with some rough synonyms). That is generally just what we want a dictionary for when we consult one. But, as Wittgenstein also pointed out, it isn't only having the examples but knowing how to extrapolate from them—knowing "how to go on"—that does the work; and that kind of knowledge dictionaries don't provide or even purport to.

Even if lots of concepts did have definitions, there couldn't, barring circularity, be definitions for *every* concept; so what is one to do about the semantics of the "primitive" concepts in terms of which the others are defined? This question is urgent because, if it isn't answered, it is easy to trivialize the claim that the sense of a concept is the property that is shared by all and only things in its extension. It is, after all, just a truism that being green is the very property that all and only (actual or possible) green things have in common, namely, the property of being green. Likewise, there is a property that all and only actual and possible cats share: the property of being a cat; likewise, there is a property that is common to all and only Sunday afternoons: the property of being Sunday afternoons; likewise, for that matter, there is a property that all and only Ulysses S. Grants share: the property of being Ulysses S. Grant. If the thesis that concepts are definitions is to be of any substance, such vacuous definitions must somehow be ruled out. Presumably that requires deciding which concepts are primitive (hence undefined) and what makes primitive concepts primitive. But, in fact, nobody knows how to answer either question.

Here's one suggestion we've heard: The primitive concepts are such very general ones as PHYSICAL OBJECT, EVENT, PROPERTY, etc.[14] But this seems to beg the question at issue since, presumably, PHYSICAL OBJECT has an extension too, so the question arises: what do the actual and possible things in its extension have in common? (It seems not to help to say that the intension of PHYSICAL OBJECT is something that is physical and an object, since this raises the question what the intensions of *those* concepts are.) Nor does the dilemma's other horn seem more attractive, namely that PHYSICAL OBJECT can be defined and so isn't primitive. For example, perhaps something is a physical object in virtue of its having a "closed shape," and/or a "continuous trajectory in space," etc. (this notion has come to be called a "Spelke Object" because it was first "defined" by Spelke [1990]). We've tried hard, but without success, to convince ourselves that the concept of a TRAJECTORY is more basic than the concept of a PHYSICAL OBJECT; isn't it true by definition that a trajectory is the path of an (actual or possible) physical object through space? We will tell you (in chapter 3) what we think a physical object is; but what we'll offer isn't (and doesn't purport to be) a definition; and, very likely, you will find our account of it disappointing.

It is to be said in praise of the empiricists (Hume, for example) that they did offer a serious suggestion about how to deal with this complex of worries. According to their "empiricist principle," all concepts reduce, via their definitions, to sensory/

experiential concepts. Accordingly, the primitive concepts are the sensory/experiential ones. But, of course, this is a principled answer to "Which concepts are primitive?" only if there is a principled answer to "Which concepts are sensory/experiential?" "Classical" Empiricism thought that there is such an answer: roughly, a sensation is a mental object such that you have one if and only if you believe that you do.[15] When taken together with the claim that sensory definability is the general case for concepts that aren't primitive, that provided empiricists with their purported refutation of skepticism; if all your concepts are directly or indirectly sensory, and if your sensory beliefs about your current sensations aren't subject to error, then contrary to what skeptics say, it follows that at least some of your beliefs about things-in-the-world (tables and chairs and the like) are certainly true.

But according to the empiricists' kind of semantic theory, intensions determine extensions; and, these days, it's hard to believe that, in the general case, things fall in the extensions of concepts in virtue of their sensory properties (that is, in virtue of how they look, sound, feel, or taste and so forth). Maybe that works for GREEN (though that it does is capable of being doubted). But it quite clearly doesn't work for CAT or PLUMBER (or for PHYSICAL OBJECT, come to think of it). Moreover, if it's true that there are very few bona fide definitions, there are still fewer bona fide *sensory* definitions. It is rare for things to fall under a concept because they satisfy a sensory definition (except, maybe, sensations). Being a cat isn't the same property as being cat shaped, cat colored, and/or being disposed to make catlike noises. We wouldn't be cats even if we were all of those.

As for us, we're not at all sure that refuting skeptics is a project that's worth the effort. Why exactly does it matter whether or not it is, in some tortured sense of the term, 'possible' that there are no tables or chairs or elephants or trees, given that, as a matter of fact, there are perfectly clearly lots of each? In any case, nothing further will be said about skepticism in this book.

One more objection to the theory that concepts are definitions: if they were, they couldn't be learned. Consider the paradigm of a definition, 'Bachelors are unmarried men'. Presumably it entails that the concept BACHELOR is the very same one as the concept UNMARRIED MAN; so it entails that to learn BACHELOR is (at a minimum) to learn that bachelors are unmarried men. But, by assumption, BACHELOR and UNMARRIED MAN are the very same concept. So, on the assumption that learning a word is learning its definition, it follows that you can't learn the concept BACHELOR unless you already have the concept UNMARRIED MAN (and, of course, vice versa). So you can't learn the concept BACHELOR (or UNMARRIED MAN) at all. This consequence (sometimes known as "Fodor's paradox") is patently intolerable. (There is a way out of it, as we'll see in later chapters. But it is very expensive; it requires abandoning the notion that concepts have intensions.)

It is essential, in thinking about the line of argument just sketched, to keep in mind the distinction between concept learning, which adds a new concept to one's prior conceptual repertoire, and word learning, which merely provides a new term with which to express a concept. It's easy to conflate the two, but doing so leads to disaster.[16] There's a heuristic that helps to keep the distinction between concepts and definitions clear: test for symmetry. Consider, once again, 'Bachelors are unmarried men'. Since the definition of a term is synonymous with the term, then if learning that the definition of 'bachelor' is 'unmarried man' and learning that bachelors are unmarried men is the way one acquires the concept BACHELOR, it follows that learning that unmarried men are bachelors is a way of acquiring the concept UNMARRIED MAN. But, clearly, you can't learn UNMARRIED MAN that way unless you already have the concept BACHELOR, which, according to the definition, *is* the concept UNMARRIED MAN. The moral: definitions are about words, not about concepts. What with one thing and another, the mainstream opinion in philosophy and cognitive science these days is that the definitional theory of conceptual content isn't true.

Concepts as Stereotypes

Just as the sheer scarcity of good examples was a primary cause of so many cognitive scientists abandoning the definitional model of concepts, it is a primary cause of the current enthusiasm for the suggestion (endorsed by many people, including Rosch, Mervis, Gray, Johnson, and Boyes-Braem 1976) that concepts are stereotypes; there are plenty of good examples of those; see, for example, Fodor 1998. Moreover, while there are relatively few cases of reliable effects of a subject's knowledge of definitions on the sorts of experimental tasks that cognitive psychologists like to use to measure cognition, such effects are easy to elicit when the manipulated variable is the extent to which a stimulus is "similar enough" to the stereotype of the category that the stimulus belongs to.[17] In effect, the difference between stereotype theories of concepts and definition theories is that whereas satisfying its definition is said to be necessary and sufficient for falling under a concept, similarity to its stereotype is said only to be sufficient.

There are, in fact, large effects of stereotypy on many standard tests of concept possession: the strength of associations (if you are asked for an example of an animal, you are much more likely to respond 'dog' than 'weasel'. Very likely that's because

DOG is a stereotype for ANIMAL and weasels aren't very similar to dogs. Likewise, there are large effects of stereotypy on reaction times in identification tasks (dogs are more quickly recognized as dogs than weasels are recognized as weasels); on "inter-judge reliability" (we are more likely to agree about whether a dog is an animal than about whether a germ is); stereotypy is an even better predictor of how early a word is learned than the frequency with which it occurs in utterances; the probability that a property of a stimulus will generalize to others stimuli of the same kind is higher when the stimulus is a stereotypic instance of a kind than when it isn't. A subject who is told that sparrows have a ten-year life span and then asked whether starlings do is more likely to guess 'yes' than a subject who is told that starlings have a ten-year life span and then asked to guess whether sparrows do. And so on. These sorts of effects generally persist when "junk variables" are controlled. In short, effects of stereotypy on subjects' behaviors are widespread and reliable; this finding is about as certain as the facts of cognitive psychology ever get. The open question, then, is not whether subjects often know which stimuli are stereotypic of their kinds; it's whether stereotypes have the properties that concepts need to have. And they clearly don't.

To begin with their virtues: stereotypy is a graded notion; things can be more or less stereotypic of a kind. A dog is more stereotypic of ANIMAL than is a pig; a pig is more stereotypic of ANIMAL than is a weasel; a weasel is a much more stereotypic ANIMAL than is a paramecium; and so on. Indeed, a thing that is pretty stereotypic of one of the kinds that it belongs to can be far less stereotypic of another. A chicken is a reasonably good example of something to have for supper, but it's only a so-so example of a bird. Like the relative ubiquity of stereotype effects, all this argues for the thesis that concepts are stereotypes at least in contrast to a theory that says they are definitions. It is something of an embarrassment for the definition story that weasels are less good examples of animals than dogs; either weasels satisfy a putative definition of ANIMAL or they don't; either they are in the extension of ANIMAL or they aren't. The definitional theory offers no account of why that should be so. (Likewise for vague concepts, marginal instances of concepts, and so on.) Because stereotype theories prefer graded parameters to dichotomies, they have no principled problem with such facts.[18]

A question in passing: Standard semantic theory has it that intensions determine extensions. Does the stereotype theory agree with that or not? That depends, of course, on what 'determine' means. A definition determines an extension in the sense that it is true of all and only the things in the concept's extension. If 'bachelor' means 'unmarried man', then all and only unmarried men are in its extension. That, however, isn't the way stereotypes work. Rather, the extension of a stereotype is usually said to be the set of things that are "sufficiently similar" to the stereotype;[19] and it is left open what sufficient similarity consists in. Indeed, what sufficient similarity consists in is different from concept to concept and context to context.[20] The way that kings are similar to one another is quite different from the way that oboes or crickets are. That's why it is natural for stereotype theorists to speak of a stereotype as a (more or less definite) location in a "multidimensional" similarity space, where different concepts correspond to different locations on what may or may not be dimensions of the same space.[21]

In any case, concepts can't be stereotypes. The argument that they can't is surprisingly straightforward: If concepts are stereotypes, stereotypes have to compose; if stereotypes don't compose, the productivity of concepts defies explanation. But (unlike definitions), stereotypes don't compose. Here's the classic example: there are stereotypic fish—trout, as it might be. (Bass and flounders aren't, perhaps, very similar to trout, but let's assume they are adequately similar for the purposes at hand. Certainly trout and bass are more similar to each other than either is to a rock or a tree.) Likewise, there are stereotypic pets; dogs win by miles with cats a bad second. But, crucially, the stereotypic pet fish isn't either a dog or a cat, it's (maybe) a goldfish. It is utterly clear that there is no general way to compute the stereotype structure of compound nouns, adverbially modified verbs, and so on, from the stereotype structures of their constituents. (Compare, for example, PET FISH with SUGAR SUBSTITUTE: a pet fish is a fish, but a sugar substitute isn't sugar.)

The cognitive science literature offers various rebuttals to this line of argument; but none of them strikes us as remotely convincing. A standard suggestion is that the function of stereotypes is heuristic: suppose that you have the concepts F and G, and your task is to understand the concept AN F THAT IS G. Pretty generally, it's safe to assume that 'F that is G' applies to, and only to, things in the intersection of F and G. But, as we've just been seeing, that doesn't hold if concepts are identified with stereotypes: paradigmatic pets aren't fish and paradigmatic fish aren't pets. This looks to us like a conclusive argument against the thesis that concepts are stereotypes, but there is a way out that is widely credited: think of stereotypes as defaults; if you don't know what Fs that are Gs are like, then bet that they are like stereotypic Fs and/or stereotypic Gs.

There is, however, a lot wrong with that suggestion. For one thing, it recommends bad bets. You would be ill advised to put a lot of money on Martian fauna being very like our fauna; or on the likelihood that the paradigmatic Roman citizen commuted to work in much the same way we do (viz. by bus or subway); or that winter at the North Pole is much like winter around here; and so on. In fact, experimental studies show that the more subjects are aware that they don't know much about Fs that are Gs, the less they are willing to bet that 'stereotypic Fs are Gs' is the general case. (Subjects who are prepared to bet that carrots are orange are measurably less willing to bet that Alaskan carrots are.) This is entirely sensible of them. 'Stereotype' is a statistical notion; and, where the standard deviation of a distribution is large, the mode is a bad predictor.

In any event, we think that the compositionality problem has been quite generally misconstrued in the cognitive science literature because it is regularly taken for granted (without argument) that the appropriate context for raising semantic issues is in theories about language—in particular, theories about linguistic communication—rather than in theories about thought. Consider a case where a pet fish problem might arise: Smith says that he is terrified of pet fish. Jones is puzzled: "Why should anyone be scared of them? Pet fish are generally (and correctly) supposed to be innocuous." Various possibilities might suggest themselves: Perhaps it's something in Smith's childhood; maybe he was once bitten by a rabid goldfish. Or possibly Smith doesn't know which kinds of fish are kept as 'pet fish'; he thinks that a lot of pet fish are piranhas. Or perhaps (less plausibly if Smith is a fluent speaker) he doesn't understand that the form of words 'pet fish' applies to all and only pets that are fish. In any event, Jones has to figure out what Smith means by 'pet fish' and, in the last case, this is plausibly a fact about the semantics of English. Our point, however, is that the Smith-and-Jones case is very unlike the ones that arise in considering the psychology of thought. Suppose Smith thinks (in whatever language he thinks in) 'That is a pet fish', and decides, accordingly, to flee. What can't be going on is that Smith thinks (the Mentalese equivalent of) 'That is a pet fish' and then asks himself 'I wonder what I meant by 'pet fish' when I thought that?' For Smith–Jones communication to occur, Jones has to figure out what Smith was thinking of when he said what he did; but Smith doesn't have to figure out what he himself was thinking about when he thought to himself 'That's a pet fish'. Accordingly, it's at least arguable that, in figuring out what Smith meant, Jones consults a semantics of English to which he and Smith both have access; Smith uses it to translate his thought into English, Jones uses it to reconstruct Smith's thought from Smith's English utterance. But, to repeat, that's about interpreting Smith's utterance. But Smith doesn't interpret his own thought; Smith just has it. And Jones doesn't interpret Smith's *thought* either; he only needs to interpret Smith's *utterance*: that is, he figures out which thought Smith intended the utterance to convey.

We think these sorts of reflections have implications for cognitive psychology. First: so far at least, the theory of linguistic communication may well require postulating an internal representation of English semantics as part of its story about how English speakers communicate in a language they share. But we doubt that there's any reason at all to suppose that thinkers resort to a semantic theory of Mentalese when they use Mentalese to think in. Tokens of Mentalese are, to be sure, "in the heads" of thinkers; and Mentalese had better have a semantics in the sense that there had better be indefinitely many truths about what a creature is thinking when he thinks something in Mentalese. But it's far from obvious that an internal representation of Mentalese semantics needs to play any role in the psychology of thinking. In the kind of referential-causal semantics we think is appropriate for Mentalese, it doesn't.

Data about how subjects construe English 'pet fish' sentences make it clear that subjects use background information in interpreting tokens of them. But that hasn't any obvious bearing on whether the constituents of the subject's thoughts are stereotypes. If that's right, then the experimental data that have generally been taken to bear on what conceptual content is are simply beside the point: they invariably are data about how subjects interpret tokens of such forms of words as 'pet fish', not data about how the conceptual constituents of their thoughts mentally represent pets or fish. Perhaps all that's going on in such experiments is that, when someone uses 'pet fish' to say something about a pet fish, it is likely to be a typical pet fish (rather than a stereotypic pet fish, or still less, each and every pet fish) that he intends to speak about. The moral such experiments point to would then be that it's a mistake to confound a theory of communication with a theory of conceptual content. More on such matters in chapter 3.

Digression

Concepts aren't the only kinds of mental representations; there are also thoughts (roughly, mental representations that express propositions). But, though our discussion has had many things to say about concepts, it has thus far said very little about thoughts. That wasn't an accident. The tradition in cognitive psychology—especially in associationistic cognitive psychology—has consisted, in large part, of not noticing the concept–thought distinction; and it has suffered for failing to do so. Before we proceed to consider "neural network" theories of conceptual content, we want to enumerate some of the differences between concepts and thoughts.

Suppose the content of one's concept WATER is (partially) constituted by the associative connection WATER → WET (that is, by the fact that mental tokens of the former regularly cause mental tokens of the latter). Still, as Kant and Frege both very rightly emphasized, it wouldn't be possible to identify an event of thinking the thought that water is wet with an event of first thinking the concept WATER and then (e.g., by association) thinking the concept WET. The reason it wouldn't is that, in the thought that water is wet, the property denoted by WET is predicated of the stuff denoted by WATER; 'water is wet' has, as one says, the "logical form" of an attribution of wetness to water. Accordingly, that thought is true or false depending on whether the stuff in question (viz., water) has the property in question (viz., being wet), which (putting ice cubes, steam, and powdered water to one side) it generally does.[22] By contrast, to associate WET with WATER is just to have tokenings of the concept WATER reliably cause tokenings of the concept WET.

Associative ("Semantic") Networks

Imagine a cognitive scientist who holds that the content of a concept is that it's a position in a network of associations; perhaps he says that the concept DOG is the position in such a network that has the associative connections: DOG → ANIMAL; DOG → BARK; DOG → BITE; DOG → CAT; DOG → DOG FOOD; and so on. Suppose he also holds that some such network of associative connections is (or determines) the content of the concept DOG. And suppose that, in his enthusiasm, he adds that the life of the mind—in particular the thinking of thoughts—consists in the excitation of such interconceptual associations. (Such theories used to be called "Connectionist," but now they have chosen to use a phrase with the connotation that the problems being studied are about the brain: connectionist graphs have become "artificial neural nets" or "ANNs.") The point we're urging is that ANNs, so construed, arrived prerefuted. *Even if concepts are states of associative networks of neurons, thinking isn't the activation of links between the nodes in such networks.* This is a problem for ANN theorists because the question of what conceptual content is and the question of what thinking is must certainly be very closely related: concepts are the constituents of thoughts; they're what thoughts are made of, and thoughts get their semantics from their conceptual constituents (viz. by composition). If you go wrong about what concepts are, you are also bound to go wrong about what thoughts are. And vice versa. (For a lot more on this topic, see Fodor and Pylyshyn 1988.)

In addition to giving the connectionist networks a biological connotation, ANNs also encourage confounding associating with thinking. Still, it's conceivable that we're wrong; so suppose, for the sake of the discussion, that we agree to "bracket" the question of what thoughts are made of. In that case, the residual question nonetheless can still be raised: "What can be said about the ANN theory of conceptual content if we decide to just not worry about what an ANN or connectionist theory of concepts would imply for a theory of thinking?" This question is important if only because ANN is just Empiricism with a degree in computer science, and Empiricism of any sort is a debilitating kind of affliction.

So, theories about thoughts to one side, consider the question of whether concepts are locations in a network of associations, and hence whether one might represent a mind's "conceptual repertoire"—the totality of concepts available to the mind at a given time—as a graph consisting of finitely many labeled nodes with paths connecting some of them to some others.[23] On the intended interpretation, the label on a node tells you which concept it stands for and the length of the lines between them (or some other graphical representation of the "weight" or impedance/gain attributed to the connection represented by the line segment) varies inversely with the strength of the association between the concepts.

So, for example, imagine a mind that has the concept RED and the concept TRIANGLE but never happens to think a thought about red triangles. Given its conceptual repertoire, such a mind could think such a thought; but, for some reason, it happens not to have done so. Does this mean that the conceptual repertoire of that mind is finite? Because connectionists/associationists don't ask this question, they haven't needed to face up to the fact that concepts are productive.

People who work with either ANNs or connectionist graphs assume that representations of different objects (or more accurately of different conceptualizations) are constituted by differences in these nets. What kind of differences? Well, primarily differences in their topology (which nodes a particular node is connected to), and in particular which nodes outside a particular subnet they are connected to (such as which external object or property they 'connect' to via a transducer). The identity of a particular network also depends on the differences among the 'weights' on each connection and the threshold of each node or 'neuron'. Figure 2.1 is an (entirely hypothetical) representation of what might be a very small part of an ANN graph of the structure of the associative relations among concepts in someone's 'associative space'. In this figure, nodes are labeled according to the features and relations that they represent. But how does this node information get into the network (how does the network know what the nodes refer to)? Wasn't that the problem we started with?

Now consider the theory that says the content of a labeled node is (or supervenes on) its connections alone. But its connections to what? The theory is that the content of a labeled node is its connections to other labeled nodes. Since the label of a node expresses its content, that would beg the very question that connectionism claims to answer: "What determines what content (i.e., what label) a node has?" Rather, the idea must be that corresponding nodes in isomorphic graphs have the same content whatever the labels of their connected nodes may be. That would avoid the threatened circularity, but it surely can't be true. It is perfectly possible, for example, that the concept ROUND has the same location on one graph as the concept SQUARE does on some isomorphic graph. If that's the situation, then according to the present way of understanding the graphs (as unlabeled), the ROUND node location and the SQUARE node location express the same content. So there's a dilemma: if the suggestion is that two nodes stand for the same content if and only if they have the same labels, then it's circular. But if the suggestion is that two nodes stand for the same concept if and only if they are connected to the corresponding nodes in isomorphic graphs, regardless of the labels of the nodes that they are connected to, then the suggestion is false (cf. SQUARE and ROUND).[24] Quine was right when he warned (in his iconic 1951 article, "Two Dogmas of Empiricism") that the familiar theories of meaning run in circles, hence that meaning should be viewed as a suspect notion for purposes of serious theory construction. That is a claim we will endorse in chapter 3.

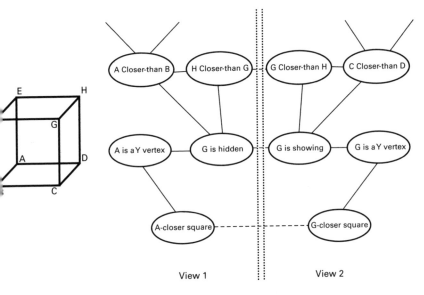

Figure 2.1

This figure illustrates a network (ANN or connectionist) in which nodes are labeled according to the features or the objects to which they refer. In this case it also shows that there are two possible representations, corresponding to the two possible views of the ambiguous drawing (based on Feldman and Ballard 1982, as redrawn in Pylyshyn 2001).

Even if it were true that node A in one graph must have the same content as node B in another graph if they have the same associative connections to corresponding nodes in isomorphic graphs, it would be of no use when the project is to explain what identity/difference of content is, because the notion of identity of labels just *is* the notion of identity of content, and, as far as we know, connectionists/associationists have no theory of conceptual content. It has been our practice to begin our discussion of each possible theory of conceptual content by enumerating its virtues. But we don't think that associationist/connection-ist accounts of content have any virtues to enumerate, except that, since associative and connective relations are both causal by definition, they have a head start over many other kinds of semantics in that they aspire to being naturalizable.[25]

Concepts as Inferential Roles

The idea here is that the content of a concept is (or supervenes on) its inferential connections, where inferential connections are not assumed to be associative. Following the literature, we call this sort of proposal an "inferential role semantics" (IRS). Versions of IRS are widespread in current philosophical theories of meaning, where it is sometimes taken to accord with Wittgen-stein's suggestion that meaning is use.

The modern history of IRS starts with Sellars's (1963) obser-vation that the content of the "logical constants" can be speci-fied by their roles in inference. AND, for example, is the concept whose inferential role is constituted by the "introduction rule" P, Q → P&Q and the "elimination rule" P&Q → P; P&Q → Q. It is, however, far from clear how the content of the concept AND might serve as a model for, say, the content of the concept TREE. In classical versions of semantic theory, the content (i.e., inten-sion) of a concept is what determines its extension, the set of things the concept applies to. But AND, unlike TREE, doesn't apply to anything; 'the set of ands' is, to put it mildly, not well defined. So it's a puzzle how the semantics of AND could provide a model of the semantics of TREE (or vice versa); in particular, it's a puzzle how the content of TREE could be determined by the rules for its use in anything like the way that introduction/elimination rules might be thought to determine the content of AND. There is a tendency (very unfortunate, from our perspective) to force the analogy by saying that, in the case of TREE, the "rules of use" are procedures for applying the concept correctly, namely, for applying it to trees. So, on close examination, IRS often proves to be yet another kind of verificationism.

All the same, the idea of constructing a theory of content based on inferential relations rather than associative relations may seem prima facie plausible; on the face of it, association doesn't seem much like thinking; nobody could seriously hold that associating CAT with DOG is tantamount to thinking that cats are dogs since, unlike thoughts, associations are neither true nor false.

There are also a number of other respects in which IRS might be able to cope with problems that give other kinds of semantic theories nightmares. Consider concepts that have empty extensions; these include, we suppose, not just AND (see above) but also SANTA CLAUS, THE NEXT EVEN PRIME AFTER TWO, GOD, GHOST, SQUARE CIRCLE, and so on. But though they lack extensions, many empty concepts appear to have contents at least in the sense that there is a story about the sorts of things that they *purport* to apply to. And it's true, more or less, that people who have the concepts generally know the corresponding stories. Maybe, then, the contents of empty concepts can be identified with their inferential roles in the corresponding stories. We think that there is something right about this view of empty concepts, but that it offers no comfort to IRS. (More on this in chapter 5.)

For those and other reasons, IRS is often the semantic theory of choice for philosophers and cognitive psychologists who like idea that the content of concepts is somehow determined by their connectivity, but who understand that association can't be the kind of connectivity that's required. But, agreeable or otherwise, it won't do.

What's Wrong with IRS?

If you want to hold that conceptual content supervenes on inferential roles, you must find some way to say which contents supervene on which roles.[26] There are, we think, only two principled options: you can say that every inference that a concept is involved in is constitutive of its content; or you can say that only some such inferences are. In the latter case, you are obliged to explain, for each concept, the difference between the inferences that are constitutive and the inferences that aren't. We are convinced that both these options invite catastrophe—indeed, that both demand it.

The First Option: Holism

Suppose that last Tuesday you saw a butterfly between your house and the one next door. Doing so adds a cluster (in fact, quite a large cluster) of new beliefs to the ones that you previously had: I saw a butterfly; I saw a butterfly between my house and the one next door; there was a butterfly visible from my house yesterday; there were butterflies around here yesterday; the total of my lifetime butterfly sightings has increased by one; there was something between my house and the one next door yesterday that probably wasn't there last January; if I hadn't been home yesterday, I likely would not have seen a butterfly; and so forth, and so on and on. And each belief adds a corresponding new rule of inference to those that you were previously wont to apply in the course of your reasoning: If yesterday was the fourth of the month, infer I saw an insect on the fourth of the month; since butterflies are insects, infer that there was an insect visible to me on the fourth of the month; and so on, depending on how far the effects that adding a new belief to one's stock of standing beliefs directly or indirectly alters the inferences to which one is committed. So, if holism is true, and every inference that a concept is involved is meaning constitutive, then the content of one's concepts alters as fast as one's beliefs do; which is to say, instant by instant.

A plethora of crazy consequences follow. Suppose yesterday you and your spouse agreed that butterflies are aesthetically pleasing; and suppose that one or the other (but not both) of you comes to believe that he/she just saw a butterfly. Conceptual holism says that you can't now so much as think the proposition about which you used to agree about, since you no longer share the concept BUTTERFLY that you used to agree on. That sort of thing can be very hard on relationships.

The natural reply to this objection is, of course, that, though the content of your concepts (hence of your beliefs) changes instant by instant, it doesn't usually change very much. But how much is that? And in what direction do one's concepts change when one's beliefs do? If the day before yesterday you believed that the Sun is a considerable distance from New Jersey, and if yesterday you came to believe that you saw a butterfly, what belief does the belief about the distance to the Sun change into? This is a morass from whose boundaries no traveler has so far returned. We very strongly recommend that you stay out of it.

The Second Option: Analyticity

The truth-values of propositions are connected to one another in all sorts of ways. For example, if P and P → Q are true, so too is Q. If 'this is a butterfly' is true, so too is 'this is an insect'. If 'my house is near your house' is true, so too is 'your house is near my house'. (On the other hand, even if my house is near your house, and your house is near John's house, my house may not be near

John's house.) If 'this glass is full of H_2O' is true, so too is 'this glass is full of water'. If 'all swans are white' is a law of nature, then 'if this had been a swan, it would have been white' is true. But nothing of the sort follows from 'all the swans I've seen so far are white'. And so on.

For all sorts of reasons, it is often of great interest to know which propositions have truth-values that are interdependent, sometimes because our well-being may rest on it, but often enough just because we're curious. Accordingly, one of the things our cognitive processes permit us to do is trace such connections; having gotten hold of one bit of the web of beliefs, we can follow it to other ones to which it's inferentially connected. We can, of course, never know about all of the inferential connections there are; nor would we conceivably wish to. But, from time to time, we can know about some of the ones that our well-being depends on, or that our curiosity leads us to look into. That's what logic and science and mathematics and history are for. That's what thinking is for.

If we can't, even in principle, know all the connections among beliefs, maybe we can know all of the *kinds* of connections that there are? Or all of the important kinds? In effect, the empiricist tradition made two epistemological suggestions about the structure of the web of beliefs, both of which have seemed plausible in their time and the first of which chapters 4 and 5 will explore: that propositions whose truth-values are accessible to perception have a special role to play in finding one's way through the web; and that all propositions have their truth-values either in virtue of their content alone or in virtue of their content together with facts about the world. The second of these is of special epistemological interest because, if there are propositions that are true or false just in virtue of their content and however the world is, there are at least some fixed points in the tangle of connections of which the web is constituted. If (or to the extent that) the content BACHELOR fixes the truth-value of 'if John is a bachelor, John is unmarried', then we can always and everywhere rely on that inference being sound, whichever of our other beliefs we may have to alter. That's to say: if there are propositions that are true in virtue of their meanings alone, and if the content of a proposition is its inferential role, then holism is false.

Call beliefs whose content doesn't depend on one's other beliefs "analytic." Convenient as a substantive notion of analyticity might be as an antidote to holism, there are an increasing number of reasons why most philosophers have ceased to believe that such a notion can be sustained.

1. The first worry is that, by assumption, analytic beliefs can't be revised without changing the content of (some or all of) their conceptual constituents; that is, they can't be changed without equivocating. But there don't seem to be any beliefs that one can't (reasonably) revise under sufficient pressure from data and background theories. The trouble is that belief change is conservative: if enough rests on a belief, and if there is some replacement for it waiting in the wings, then any belief may be rationally abandoned, even the ones that are allegedly analytic.

2. The second worry is that you can't use the notion of analyticity to explicate the notion of meaning, content, intension, or any of the others that are central to semantics, on pain of begging the questions that semantics is supposed to answer; otherwise, since analyticity is itself a semantic notion par excellence, you end up in a circle.

Both these lines of argument were spelled out in Quine's paper "Two Dogmas of Empiricism" (Quine 1951); nor, to our knowledge, has either been seriously rebutted.

The moral of this chapter is that all the available accounts of conceptual content (or, anyhow, all the ones we've heard of) seem to be pretty clearly not viable; we think that those who cling to them do so mostly in despair. At a minimum, it seems to us that the arguments against the available theories of content are sufficiently impressive that it would be unwise to take senses, intensions, or the like for granted in any semantic theory of content that you care about, theories of the semantics of mental representations very much included. So, what now?

Why, after all these years, have we still not caught sight of the Loch Ness Monster? Of course, it might be that we've been looking in the wrong places. We're told that Loch Ness is very large, very deep, and very wet; and we believe all of that. But, as the failures pile up, an alternative explanation suggests itself: The reason we haven't found the Loch Ness Monster is that there is no such beast.

Likewise, we think, in semantics: the reason that nobody has found anything that can bear the weight that meaning has been supposed to bear—it determines extensions, it is preserved under translation and paraphrase, it is transmitted in successful communication, it is what synonymy is the identity of, it supports a semantic notion of necessity, it supports philosophically interesting notions of analytic necessity and conceptual analysis, it is psychologically real, it distinguishes among coextensive concepts (including empty ones), it is compositional, it is productive, it isn't occult, and, even if it doesn't meet quite all of those criteria, it does meet a substantial number—the reason that meaning has proved so elusive is that there is no such beast as that either. We think that, like the Loch Ness Monster, meaning is a myth.

The rest of the book is about how it might be possible to construct a semantics for mental representations that is reasonably plausible, sufficient for the purposes of cognitive science, and compatible with naturalistic constraints on empirical explanations, but which dispenses with the notion of meaning altogether: it recognizes reference as the only relevant factor of content. Accordingly, although there are plenty of extensions, they aren't determined by intensions. We don't claim to know for sure that any such theory is viable; and, even assuming that some or other is, we don't claim to know, in any detail, how to arrive at it. But maybe we can point in the right general direction.

Appendix: Semantic Pragmatism

We have disagreed, in one way or another, with each of the theories of conceptual content discussed in this chapter.[27] But they all share a premise that we fully endorse: concepts are identified, at least in part, by their relations to thoughts. We think this is true in a number of respects: concepts function as the constituents of thoughts; the same concept (type) can be a constituent of indefinitely many different thoughts; minds that share a concept may disagree about the truth (or falsity) of indefinitely many of the thoughts of which that concept is a constituent; and so on. One might suppose that, if anything in semantic theory is "true by definition," that premise is. So why do so many philosophers (and so many others) reject it?

At least since Wittgenstein advised that we ask for the use of symbols rather than their meanings, semanticists have often been attracted by the more or less pragmatist thesis that there is an intrinsic connection between a concept's content and its role in the integration and/or causation of behavior. Prinz and Clark (2004; henceforth P&C) put it this way: to "sever ... putatively constitutive links between thinking and any kind of doing is ...

a doctrine that we should not seriously contemplate, on pain of losing our grip on what concepts are for, and why we bother to ascribe them" (57). We don't know whether this anxiety is justified because, of course, nobody ever has suggested the severing of concepts from actions; certainly not the present authors. What has been widely suggested—and what we think is true—is that the connection between concepts and actions is invariably contingent; in particular, it is not constitutive of conceptual content. Rather, the connections between the concepts that a creature has and the behavior it performs is invariably mediated by what the creature thinks and what it wants. Ever since Aristotle invented the "practical syllogism" (see above), and excepting only behaviorists, the consensus has been that what creatures do depends on their beliefs and desires.

That view is, of course, fully compatible with taking concepts to be individuated by reference to their roles as constituents of propositional attitudes: you can't want to eat an apple unless you have the concept APPLE. Representational theories of mind say that's because wanting to eat an apple involves being related, in the appropriate way, to a mental representation of how things would be if you got what you want. Notice that that claim is not the one that P&C (or other neopragmatists) dispute. Rather, pragmatism is about whether the concept APPLE is somehow constituted by its role in "action-oriented" behaviors, among which eating apples would presumably be included. According to Aristotle, that's because lots of people who have the concept APPLE believe that they are good to eat; were it not that they think apples are edible, they would cease to eat them. Notice, however, that on Aristotle's view, unlike the pragmatist's, it is extremely plausible that one's APPLE concept would survive abandoning one's belief that apples are edible, even though apple-eating behaviors would not. That is part of the explanation of why an argument between someone who thinks that apples are poisonous and someone who doesn't, isn't, as one says, "merely verbal." If you think eating apples makes one sick and I don't, our disagreement isn't about the concept APPLE (or the word 'apple'); it's about whether eating apples makes one sick. It was a *discovery* that apples are good to eat, not a semantic stipulation. Ask Eve.

Now P&C have, of course, every right not to believe that. They might hold—perhaps on Quine–Duhem grounds—that there just isn't any principled way to distinguish what one knows in virtue of having the concept APPLE from what one knows in virtue of knowing what apples are good for. Our point, however, is that you can't (and Quine–Duhem don't) defend such claims by saying that unless EDIBLE is constitutive of APPLE, the connection between thinking about apples and eating them is somehow severed. One doesn't need to turn pragmatist to avoid severing such connections; all one need do is to hold that they are causal (hence contingent) rather than semantic (hence necessary).

We do agree that there's a problem about how to distinguish beliefs about the intensions of concepts from beliefs about the things in their extensions. As will presently become apparent, that's one of the reasons we think that individuating concepts by their intensions is a mistake. But, whether or not we're right about that, pragmatism doesn't help to solve the problem of concept individuation, since if identifying concepts by their relation to thoughts would sever their connection to actions, identifying concepts by their relations to actions would sever their connection to thoughts; and severing the connections between concepts and thoughts would be a disaster, since concepts are the constituents of thoughts. The concept APPLE is a constituent both of the thought that apples are good to eat and of the thought that they aren't.

Apple-thoughts are, quite generally, connected to apple-actions by more or less complicated chains of inference, among the premises of which there are, almost invariably, some that are contingent. (Among these, in the present case, is the proposition that eating apples makes you sick.) But how could that be so if, as pragmatists hold, the connection between conceptual contents and actions is constitutive of the concept's identity? P&C never do try to cope with this (perfectly standard) kind of objection to pragmatism. Instead they suggest that we consider the concept of a 50-pound egg. Very well, then; let's.

P&C tell us that, unless we keep it in mind that the mothers of 50-pound eggs are sure to be very large and likely to be very fierce, we are at risk of having serious trouble with the creatures that lay them. But though that is certainly true, we don't think that keeping it in mind is a condition for grasping the concept of a 50-pound egg. Rather, we think that the content of the concept 50-POUND EGG is just: egg that weighs 50 pounds. This is demanded by the view, which we likewise endorse (idioms and the like aside), that the content of complex concepts is determined by composition from the content of their constituents. So, which of its constituent concepts do P&C suppose contributes the content *dangerous* to the content of the concept MOTHER OF A 50-POUND EGG? Is it MOTHER, perhaps?

What leads us to give creatures that lay 50-pound eggs a wide berth is: putting the content of the concept together with what we know (or surmise) about a 50-pound egg's likely parentage (and with a lot of other stuff as well). If that weren't so, we wouldn't be able to so much as contemplate the possibility that mothers of such very large eggs have been the victims of slander and are, as a matter of fact, as gentle as lambs. If that isn't at least conceptually possible, what on Earth could Maurice Sendak have been up to?

So why, in virtue of all the old questions that it fails to solve and all the new questions that it gratuitously invites, are there so many converts to semantic pragmatism both in philosophy and in cognitive science? To be sure, pragmatism shares with Marlboro ads a certain macho air of cutting through the frills and getting to the bare bones of doing things. "In the real world thinking is always and everywhere about doing," as P&C say. But, on reflection, that strikes us as pretty obviously untrue and, in any case, unduly dogmatic. Who knows what, if anything, thinking is always about? Or indeed, whether there is anything that thinking is always about? And anyhow, to the best of our knowledge, "The Real World" is just the world; people who rest a lot on a presumed difference between the two are almost always just bluffing.

3 Contrarian Semantics

As we understand the jargon of Wall Street, a "contrarian" is someone whose practice is to buy when everybody else sells and to sell when everybody else buys. In effect, contrarians believe that what more or less everybody else believes is false more or less all of the time. This book is an essay in contrarian semantics. Chapter 2 reviewed a spectrum of theories about the content of concepts (the 'intensions' of concepts; the 'meanings' of concepts; the 'senses' of concepts; etc.), which, though they differ in all sorts of other ways, all agree that the content of a concept is whatever determines its extension: Concepts C and C' have the same content only if (C applies to a thing if and only if C' does).

However, sticky questions arise at once. For example, is the content of concept C to be defined relative to the things that it *actually* applies to or to the things that it *would* apply to if there were such things? Philosophers love this kind of question; but in cognitive science they aren't often explicitly discussed. Our impression, for what it's worth, is that usually (but not always), it is the "modal" reading that cognitive science has in mind. Assume, for illustration, that there are no green cats. Still, the question arises whether the extension of CAT would include a green domestic feline if there chanced to be one. If your view is that the content of a concept is its *definition*, then your answer is "yes." If, however, your view is that concepts are stereotypes, the answer is less clear: it would depend on (among other things) the ratio of green cats to cats. Note that only *actual* cats need apply since there is, presumably, no bound to the number of *possible* green cats that there could be, if there could be any. We think this disagreement about modal force is the heart of the difference between stereotype theories of conceptual content and definition theories, but that's not why we raise the issue here; rather, it's to illustrate the kinds of difficulties that arise in deciding just what intensionalism amounts to; what exactly it is that the friends of intensions are required to assert and their antagonists are required to deny.

We propose to stipulate: intensions are defined by their relation to *extensions*; in particular, by the following principles:

1. Intensions *determine* extensions; that is, intensionally identical representations are ipso facto coextensive.

2. If coextensive representations are not semantically equivalent, they must be intensionally distinct.

This chapter will argue that there is nothing that satisfies both (1) and (2), and hence that there are no such things as intensions.[1] Now, in the cognitive science community at least, this view is not just contrarian, it's heretical; it's simply taken for granted that intensions (meanings, senses, etc.) satisfy (1) and (2) above. There is, however, some indication that the tide has turned in Anglophone philosophy, where versions of "causal theories" of reference are currently fashionable. We will ourselves offer one in chapters 4 and 5; but, for all sorts of reasons, it differs from the kinds that are in vogue at present. (For an

Anglophone philosopher who cleaves to the "intensions determine extensions" tradition, see, e.g., Jackson 1977.)

We start with what we will call "Frege arguments" (though we admit they may have at most a tenuous connection to arguments that the historical Frege actually endorsed).

Frege Arguments

The paradigm Frege argument is: "If meaning didn't determine reference, then coextensive words/concepts would be cointensive (in particular, coreferential words would be synonyms). But there are, according to several standard and reasonable criteria, coextensive words that are *not* synonyms. So the content of a word must consist of something more (or other) than its extension; and its intension is the only other option. The same for concepts, mutatis mutandis."

We want to meet the Frege arguments head on, so we'll just grant that, for example, 'George Washington' (hereinafter GW) and 'our first president' (hereinafter OFP), though coextensive, aren't synonyms. What shows they aren't is a line of argument that Frege relies on very heavily: substitution of one synonym for another preserves the truth/falsity of sentences and thoughts that contain them (in the philosophical jargon, synonyms substitute *salve veritate*). But substitution of coextensives need not preserve truth/falsity in propositional attitude (PA) contexts. 'John doesn't believe that GW was OFP' does not imply 'John doesn't believe that GW was GW'. So coextensives aren't, per se, synonyms.

Fair enough; let's suppose that such considerations show that coextension *isn't* sufficient for identity of content. The question is: what follows from that? In particular, how does it show that there are intensions?

There is, to begin with, more than a whiff of a missing premise here. To make this sort of argument work, an intensionalist must assume not only that 'GW' and 'OFP' are coextensive (to which historical consensus testifies) but also that if it isn't coextension that guarantees synonymy (hence substitution salve veritate), it's got to be cointension that does. But that follows only if it's also assumed that coextension and cointension are the only candidates for identification with conceptual content. What entitles intensionalists (Frege included) to assume that?

We think that Frege's sorts of examples do show that something other than mere coextensivity is required for a viable notion of conceptual (or lexical) content; but why concede that cointension is the mandatory alternative? This question is pressing if you think, as we do, that there is no plausible account of what an intension is, and (to repeat) that even if there were, nobody has the slightest idea of how intension, synonymy, and the like might be naturalized.[2] (Naturalizability, as the reader may recall, was among the working assumptions we set out in chapter 1.)

Consider, once again, John, who believes that GW was GW but does not believe that GW was OFP, so that, if you ask John who GW was (and if he is feeling compliant) he will confidently and sincerely and correctly answer that GW was GW, whereas, if you ask him who OFP was, he will confidently and sincerely and correctly answer that he doesn't know. It seems that, if coextension implies cointension, we must either hold that the substitution of cointensive terms does affect truth-value, or that (contrary to a claim to which naturalistic PA psychology is surely committed) one's beliefs aren't causes of one's behavior, question-answering behavior included. Prima facie, if Frege's sorts of examples show what intensionalists think they do, then they show either that PA psychology isn't true or that, if it is, it can't be naturalized.

If we read him right, Frege himself thought something like this: John doesn't believe that GW was OFP when he (GW) is described as (when he is 'presented under the guise of') our first president. But John does believe that GW was OFP when he (GW again) is described as GW. That's a perfectly coherent view as far as it goes; but the naturalization of belief-desire psychology requires that believing should be understood in terms of nonsemantic notions, and 'satisfied' and 'described as' and the like don't qualify. Describing something as such and such is, surely, a species of saying that it is such and such. And 'saying that' is quite as semantic as 'believing that'. So we're in a circle of interdefinitions again. So belief-desire psychology can't be naturalized.

The sound you now hear is that of indefinitely many hard-headed cognitive scientists replying that they couldn't care less who wins these word games. What they care about is, for example, how (or whether) John's beliefs cause his behavior. One can't but sympathize; but it just won't do. John does *say* that he doesn't know who OFP was, and we're taking it that he says so sincerely. Nor is this a case of, for example, behavior being driven by unconscious beliefs in the way that verbal slips are sometimes thought to be. So, if coextension entails cointension, John really does believe that GW is OFP; and his sincerely saying that he doesn't is a prima facie counterexample to belief-desire psychology in a way that his verbal slips are not. Looked at this way, the problem that John raises for belief-desire psychology isn't that it is forced to say that the belief that GW was OFP is in John's head but somehow unavailable to his introspection. It's that, for all either his introspection or his behavior shows, the belief that GW was OFP just isn't in there, either consciously or unconsciously. Even analyzing his dreams won't bring it to light. For the purposes of psychological explanation, it might just as well not be there.

Frege thought the right thing to say is that John believes that GW was OFP when GW is described as OFP, but not when GW is described as GW; a view that (as we mentioned above) is non-naturalistic in that it relies on semantic notions ('described as') to explicate a psychological notion ('believe that'). Frege doesn't mind that because he very much isn't a naturalist. He takes principles like "descriptions that are coextensive need not be synonyms" to be, as it were, at metaphysical ground level. Descriptions *just are* kinds of things that can be coextensive but not cointensive; there is nothing more to be said about that without resort to still further semantic vocabulary. But, of course, hard-headed cognitive scientists are ipso facto naturalists, and so are we. So now what?

The story we like goes something like this: the form of words (1), below, is ambiguous. It has both the reading (2) and the reading (3). The point of present interest is that, although reading (2) makes (1) false, reading (3) makes (1) true. So, on the one hand, John doesn't believe the proposition that GW was OFP; but, on the other hand, there's a reasonably robust sense in which he does believe the proposition that GW was OFP, even though he sincerely denies that he does. After all, John believes the proposition that GW was GW; and, in point of historical fact, GW was OFP.

1. John believes GW was OFP.

2. John believes of GW (when described as GW) that he was OFP.

3. GW is such that, when GW is described as OFP, John believes of him that he was OFP.

From the logico-syntactic point of view this is all unsurprising; what has happed is just that 'GW' is moved from its 'opaque' position inside the scope of 'believes' in (2) to a 'transparent' position outside the scope of 'believes' in (3). It's being in the former position renders 'GW' inferentially inert in (2) and its being in the latter position renders 'GW' inferentially active in (3). So the substitution of coextensives is valid outside the scope of PA operators but not inside the scope of PA operators. (Frege thinks that's because terms in opaque contexts denote not their extensions but their intensions. But that issue needn't concern us for present purposes.)

OK so far. Indeed, there's plenty of precedent. Compare quoted expressions: Suppose John uttered 'that man has a martini'; and suppose that, as a matter of fact, but unknown to John, the man with the martini was Abe Lincoln. Then it's unsurprising that John can perfectly sincerely, though falsely, deny that he said that Abe Lincoln has a martini. One way to put it is that, although John does believe that the martini-man was Abe, he doesn't know that he does. That's not a paradox. 'Abe is drinking a martini' follows from 'Abe is the martini-man' only given a pertinent fact to which John isn't privy, namely, that the man with the martini is Abe.

So, everything is fine: John's denying that he believes (/said) that Abe is the drinker isn't, after all, a counterexample to the very plausible claim that one's beliefs drive one's behavior. What the example does show, however, is the importance of distinguishing between 'John believes Abe is the martini-man' when Abe is so described (which is true), and 'John believes that Abe is the martini-man' when Abe is described as, for example, GW. Or, to put it still differently, the example shows that, in one sense of 'what you believe', some of what you believe depends not only on 'what's going on in your head' but also on 'what's going on in the world'. This theme will recur later in the discussion.

But though we think that some such story is likely true, we are committed naturalists, so there isn't any story of that sort that we are allowed to tell. As previously remarked, naturalists aren't allowed to use semantic vocabulary in their construal of PA explanations; and, of course, 'proposition', 'true', and 'so described' are all semantic terms par excellence. So the circularity–non-naturalizability dilemma persists in persisting. We need a naturalistic and uncircular construal of what John believes, says, and the like, but we haven't got one. So now what?

Our proposal traces back at least to Carnap (1956).[3] Here's the basic idea of Carnap's treatment: One should take very seriously the observation that names, descriptions, and the like, when in the scope of expressions like 'so described', 'as such', 'under the guise of', 'under the mode of presentation', and the like, work in much the way that quoted expressions do. To say that John believes that GW was OFP when GW is so described would be to say something like: John believes that tokens of the representation type 'GW was OFP' are true; whereas, to say that John believes that GW was GW is to say something like: John believes that tokens of the representation type 'GW was GW' are true. In effect, Carnap's idea is that quoted linguistic expressions might do much the same work that propositions are traditionally supposed to do in explicating semantic notions like conceptual content, belief, and so on. From the point of view of a logician whom the inferential inertness of PA contexts would otherwise cause to lose sleep, that suggestion might well seem plausible.

Notice, in particular, that if Carnap is right, the 'GW' in (4) refers not to the father of our country but to the form of words 'GW', which is one that is used (in English) to refer to our first president. So if what (1) means is more or less what (4) says, then it's unsurprising that (4) doesn't imply (5'), even though GW was in point of fact OFP.

4. John believes 'GW was OFP'.

5'. John believes GW was OFP.

Expressions inside quotation marks don't refer to what the same expression do when the quotation marks are removed.

We're fond of Carnap's answer to Frege's puzzle, because it invokes the independently plausible thesis that talking about beliefs is interestingly like talking about linguistic expressions. Both thoughts and sentences are, after all, systematic, productive, and compositional; and the similarity between, on the one hand, the relation of thoughts to their constituent concepts and, on the other hand, the relation of sentences to their constituent words, is surely too striking to ignore. So, just as the LOT version of RTM argues for the assimilation of mental content to linguistic content, so Carnap's account of the logic of PA contexts argues for their assimilation to quotations. Whichever way you approach it, thinking seems a lot like talking. That's perhaps unsurprising too, since we use language to say what we think. This is the way things ought to work in empirical theory construction: everybody takes in everybody else's wash. No stick can hold itself up, but every stick helps hold up every other.

But, in principle, Carnap can do without his story about PA contexts working like quotation contexts. Technical details aside, *any* cognitive theory that embraces RTM—any cognitive theory according to which the relation between minds and propositions is mediated by discursive mental representations—can resolve Frege's problem in much the same way that Carnap does, whether or not it assimilates the inferential inertness of PA contexts to that of quotation contexts. The basic point is that Frege's sorts of examples don't show what Frege thought they do: that thoughts and concepts must have intensions. The most they show is that their extensions can't be the *only* parameter along which thoughts and concepts are individuated; there must be at least one other.

Frege just took for granted that, since coextensive thoughts (concepts) can be distinct, it must be difference in their intensions that distinguish them. But RTM, in whatever form, suggests another possibility: Thoughts and concepts are individuated by their extensions *together with their vehicles*. The concepts THE MORNING STAR and THE EVENING STAR are distinct because the corresponding mental representations are distinct. That must be so since the mental representation that expresses the concept THE MORNING STAR has a constituent that expresses the concept MORNING, but the mental representation that expresses the concept THE EVENING STAR does not. That's why nobody can have the concept THE MORNING STAR who doesn't have the concept MORNING and nobody can have the concept THE EVENING STAR who doesn't have the concept EVENING.

Likewise, the thought that *Cicero was fat* and the thought that *Tully was fat* are distinct because the corresponding mental representations contain different names of Tully (i.e., of Cicero). Carnap's assimilation of PA contexts to quotation contexts is, to be sure, a special case of that sort of explanation; but he can do without it so long as he cleaves to some or other version of RTM. The serious question about inferential inertness isn't whether

PA contexts are a species of quotation contexts; it's whether you need differences among intensions to individuate concepts (thoughts), or whether differences between the morpho-syntatic forms of mental representations could do the job instead.

Here's a simple illustration: Forget about whether there are senses. Forget about the putative analogy between PA contexts and quotation contexts. For that matter, forget about whether Substitution of Identicals (SI) is valid in either context. It suffices to deal with Cicero/Tully worries to note the asymmetry in (6).

6. John believes of Cicero that Cicero/he/*Tully is coming to dinner.

The moral, to repeat, is just that Frege cases don't show what Frege took them to: They don't show that purely referential semantics can't do what a semantics is supposed to: in particular, they don't explain why SI and existential generalization fail in PA contexts. The result of Frege's missing this was a century during which philosophers, psychologists, and cognitive scientists in general spent wringing their hands about what meanings could possibly be: images, definitions, stereotypes, affordances, nodes in associative (or neural) networks, Platonic forms, motor engrams, neural engrams 'little s-r' associations, locations in semantic space, or whatever. It's hard to imagine that anybody really believes the project has been successful or that it is likely to be in any foreseeable future. We think it's time to throw in the towel.

We aren't, of course, denying that, in a rough, ready, commonsensical sort of way, communication, paraphrase, and thoughts, as well as abridgement, synopsis, and plagiarism, really happen. Of course they do. Rather, our suggestion is that none of these is the name of a 'natural kind' of semantic relation. In which case, if any version of RTM is true, there couldn't be *theories* of the translation, communication, abridgement, synopsis, etc. of thoughts in anything like the way in which there are theories of photosynthesis, or glacial drift, or (maybe) evolution. In fact, we rather think that, deep down, even for languages like English, to say nothing of LOT, nobody really thinks that there's a strict matter of fact about what is the "right" translation of a certain text; or whether two expressions are, strictly speaking, synonyms; or which of two metaphors is the better; or which of two jokes is the funnier; or whether a paraphrase misses something that's essential to a text; or what, precisely, is the message transmitted in a certain communication. Such decisions are endlessly sensitive to contextual detail; often enough they are matters of taste. (Hamlet told Ophelia to get herself to a nunnery. That puzzled Ophelia, and critics have been arguing about what he meant for five hundred years or so. The end is not in sight.) Quite probably you can't say what a good metaphor, or translation, or synopsis is in any vocabulary that's not already up to its ears in semantic notions, MEANING included, hence quite unlike, for example, the vocabulary of neural science, or of biochemistry. Compare E. O. Wilson's (2013) remarkably naïve suggestion that science and criticism might eventually team up to answer such questions once and for all.

If we're right about all that, then it's not just theories of conceptual content to which notions like translation and meaning are unavailable; they aren't available for the purposes of *any* strictly scientific and naturalistic enterprise. A serious and naturalistic theory of content might tell us what anaphora is; or what, if anything, generic nouns denote; or whether 'the' is a quantifier; or maybe even what the sufficient conditions for reference are; indeed, we think that the vindication of cognitive science requires that a serious and naturalistic theory of content do at least the third. We don't, however, expect it to tell us what a good translation of *Pride and Prejudice* is, or even which of two translations of *Pride and Prejudice* is the better one.

Where does all this leave us? There are, we think, two options: Give up on the Representational Theory of Mind (RTM) (and hence on claiming that the semantic contents of thoughts and concepts are pairs of their vehicles and their extensions); or give up on the chance of a serious account of communication, paraphrase, translation, and the like and suppose that, strictly speaking, the only kind of cognitive psychology there can be is individual psychology (much as many linguists think that the only grammars there can be are grammars of idiolects). Given what we take to be the really hopeless failure of cognitive science to devise a remotely plausible account of conceptual/lexical content, we can't in good conscience recommend that you endorse the first; but we're quite content to endorse the second.

Other Arguments against Referentialism

A scattering of other arguments have, from time to time, been said to refute the suggestion that conceptual content is purely referential. None of these goes as deep as Frege's observation that expressions in PA contexts are characteristically inferentially inert, and in particular, that substitution of otherwise coreferential expressions isn't reliably truth-preserving in such contexts. But some of them have nevertheless seemed persuasive. We're about to survey a couple of alternatives to Frege's sort of polemic against naturalistic theories of mind.[4]

"Empty" Concepts

There is no Devil and there are no unicorns; so one might reasonably claim that the concepts THE DEVIL and THE ONLY UNICORN IN CAPTIVITY are coextensive; both denote the empty set. And so too, mutatis mutandis, do the corresponding English expressions. But (so we suppose) THE DEVIL and THE ONLY UNICORN are different concepts; nor are the expressions 'the devil' and 'the only unicorn' synonymous. So, once again the conclusion: There must be more to conceptual content (/lexical meaning) than extension.

Now, we might complain that, strictly speaking, all of that is tendentious in one way or another. The inference from "The Devil' has no extension' to "The Devil' refers to the empty set' is too quick. The right thing to say about 'the Devil' isn't, perhaps, that it refers to the empty set, but that it doesn't refer at all. "Still," you might reply, "'The Devil has no manners' isn't meaningless, and it isn't a synonym of 'the only unicorn has no manners', both of which it ought to be if meaning is reference." To which we might reply: "We didn't say that meaning is reference; we said that there is no such thing as meaning." If you think this rejoinder is frivolous, we repeat: There is more to content than reference; but that doesn't, in and of itself, argue that part (still less all) of content is meaning. And, as we've been seeing, if there isn't any such thing as meaning, there can't be any such thing as synonymy, since synonymy is, by definition, identity of meaning. A fortiori there is no such thing as the synonymy of DEVIL and UNICORN. So who wins this sort of argument? Or is it a draw?

We don't think this question is "merely philosophical." But we can imagine that a hard-headed cognitive scientist might not agree. What's true, in any case, is that we have yet to explain why, even if there is no synonymy, there are more or less reliable "intuitions of synonymy." If those aren't really intuitions of identity of meaning, of what are they intuitions?[5] It's some-times suggested, in aid of "inferential role" accounts of meaning (see chapter 1), that, at a minimum, they can explain how there could be differences in content between referentially empty concepts.

Presumably anybody who knows what 'is a unicorn' means should be willing to infer that if there aren't any unicorns, then there aren't any unicorns' horns. But, because it's possible to believe in unicorns but not believe in the Devil, it's possible for someone who knows what 'devil' and 'unicorn' mean and is pre-pared to infer from 'no unicorns' to 'no unicorns' horns' never-theless refuses to infer from 'no unicorns' to 'no Devil's horns'. So, even assuming 'unicorn' and 'Devil' are coextensive (because both denote the empty set), their inferential roles (hence their meanings, according to IRS) are different. Likewise, someone who hasn't heard about the Morning Star being the Evening Star might reasonably decline the inference from 'The Morning Star is uninhabited' to 'The Evening Star is uninhabited'. By contrast, if 'bachelor' and 'unmarried man' really are synonyms, then the inference from 'is a bachelor' to 'is an unmarried man' should be accepted by anybody rational who understands both expres-sions. Arguably, the identity of meaning with inferential role would explain all these facts, whereas, prima facie, the sort of meaning nihilism that we are preaching cannot.

So far so good: if there are such things as inferential roles and if coextensive concepts (expressions) can have different inferen-tial roles, that would explain the (presumptive) intuition that coextensive concepts can differ in content. So let's suppose, for the purposes of argument, that there are such things as infer-ential roles (and that the worry, raised in chapter 1, that infer-ential role semantics is intrinsically holistic can be coped with somehow or other). In that case, there is, after all, a respectable argument for IRS, and hence for there being meanings as well as extensions. No?

No. The suggestion that meaning is inferential role is subject to the same objection as all the other stories about what meaning is that we've discussed so far; namely, that since inference is itself a semantic notion, such suggestions are circular. For example, inferring from one thought to another isn't just any old case of one thought causing another; it's a case of thought-to-thought causation that is generally truth preserving (associationists to the contrary notwithstanding). The hard part of figuring out what thinking is, is to explain why it preserves truth when it does, and why it doesn't preserve truth when it doesn't. And, of course, truth (like reference) is a paradigmatically mind–world relation.

For all that, perhaps you feel a certain nostalgia for the view that something like inferential role is preserved in translation, synonymy, paraphrase, communication, and the like. So be it. We are prepared to split the difference. What is appealing about the idea that content and IRS are somehow the same thing can be retained without construing IRS as a theory of content.

Here's the idea: matching conceptual roles are indeed what good translation etc. aims to achieve; but it isn't a supervenience base for intentional content. That's because (as previously remarked) there is no such thing as intentional content. Rather, what goes on is something like this: every concept has a (possibly null) extension; but also, each mental representation is surrounded by a (rather hazy) belt of connections between its tokenings and tokenings of other mental representations. Extensions must, of course, be preserved in translation, communication, and the like; if I ask you for a mouse, an elephant won't do; if you bring me an elephant, then you're being mean; or perhaps you don't know the difference between mice and elephants; most likely you just didn't understand the request. Likewise, a rough alignment of our conceptual roles is a desideratum in communication, translation, and the like. Perhaps I believe, and you know that I believe, that gray mice are nice on toast but brown mice are not; and suppose that I believe, and you know that I believe, that it's nearly time for lunch. None of that is plausibly part of the content of my (or of your) MOUSE concept; not, at least, if content is supposed to connect, in the usual ways, with analyticity, modality, and the like. Still, communication between us would have been less than a success if, given my preferences, and given what you believe about my preferences, and given what I believe that you believe about my preferences, and so on, you bring me a brown mouse for lunch.

We think this is the right way to think about how inferential roles connect to communication and, mutatis mutandis, to other cognitive processes that are commonly said to be meaning preserving. That would explain why such processes are so invariably vague and open ended and context sensitive—in fact, why they aren't, and quite possibly can't be, the domains of serious theories. And, we emphasize, you can have all that without supposing that there are any relations at all between inferential roles and conceptual content. Even a meaning nihilist can have all of it, for free.

We've known students to be outraged by such proposals as that there aren't any such things as translations, metaphors, communication, definitions, and so on. But, truly, we only mean the kind of thing that a botanist means by saying that there is no such thing as grass. Of course there is grass for workaday purposes; but not for the purposes of scientific taxonomy or scientific explanation, which are, as Beatrice would put it, "too costly to wear for working days."[6]

"One Over Many"

Plato worried about what it is that just acts have in common as such. (That's why he cared so much about defining 'table' and 'chair': his idea was that 'justice' and 'chair' are both grist for the philosophical mill because each applies to, and only to, things that satisfy its definition.) If so, there is after all a reasonable response to "Why do we need meanings?" Namely, it's because some truths about which properties that the things in a concept's extension have essentially are grounded in semantic truths about the concept; in effect, it's part of the meaning of 'chair' that chairs are to sit on. Metaphysics is just one damned analyticity after another.

Our reply is uncharacteristically brief: we don't believe a word of that. It is (as Kripke has remarked) typically empirical inquiry, not lexicography, that reveals essences. It was chemists who figured out the essence of water, not philosophers.

People who think that there is a semantic solution to Plato's problem about the one over the many do so because they think that "What do chairs have in common?" can be answered in a vocabulary that doesn't include 'chair' (i.e., in any such vocabulary in which the definition of 'chair' can be framed). But we doubt that there is such a vocabulary. What chairs have in common as such is that they, and only they, are chairs. Semanticists who think otherwise are cordially invited to define 'chair'. We doubt they will succeed.

Which Link?

Suppose there is a causal chain from a thing-in-the-world to a representational mental (/neural) state; and suppose (what can't but be true) that this chain has more than one link. The question arises, which link in the chain is the referent of the state? If you think that there are intensions and that intensions determine extensions, there is no problem: it's the link that satisfies the intension. George Washington is the extension of the concept GEORGE WASHINGTON because the concept GEORGE WASHINGTON is actually a description, and George Washington is the one and only thing-in-the-world that satisfies the description. Perhaps he's even the one and only thing in any *possible* world that does. But what if you don't think that there are such things as intensions?

That question is discussed (and, we think, answered) by Fodor (2009), so we won't repeat the proposal here. The general idea is that the most proximal link in a world-to-representation chain is the one at which all the actual and counterfactual chains from the world to that link intersect. (If we aren't allowed counterfactuals, we give up.) 'That chair' refers to that chair because all the causal chains that end with my having said 'that chair' did intersect (or would have) at that chair.

"But suppose there is only one such chain, actual or counterfactual? What is the referent then?" We think we're committed to the following (more or less Berkeleyan) prediction: if the actual causal chain is the only one that's possible (perhaps because a certain creature has only one sensory mechanism, or only one connection between its sensory mechanisms and its brain), then that creature can't refer to things-in-the-world (in effect, it can't see things as being-in-the-world). Roughly, a token of 'that chair' refers to that particular token chair only if, all else equal, all the causal chains that end (have ended/would have ended) in that token intersect at that chair. To be sure, it's not very obvious how such a claim might be tested; but perhaps the following datum is relevant: if the retina is "stabilized" (so that movements of the eye or of the percept always produce the proximal image of the percept at the same place on the retina and the same brain state), the percept fades. In effect, you can't refer to a thing-in-the-world that has only one way to get at your brain.

As we remarked, many people who deny that reference (even *perceptual* reference) can be naturalistically explained think that's because there's a puzzle about which link in a causal chain is the referent of a mental representation. The suggestion is that, unless there's an 'interpreter' on the scene to assign a referent to the representation, there would be 'no fact of the matter' about which link in the chain is the one that is being referred to. And, of course INTERPRETATION is itself a semantic/intensional concept and so is itself in want of naturalization (see, e.g., Dennett 1991; Davidson 1970; Quine 1960).

But we think this line of thought overlooks a plausible option, namely that the right link can be located by the (actual or counterfactual) applications of a procedure of 'triangulation'. For elaboration, see Fodor 2010, 213–215.

Those are all the non-Fregean arguments we can think of against the contrarian thesis that there is nothing to conceptual content except reference. We end the chapter with what we take to be a very powerful argument that favors it: if conceptual content is referential, the notorious 'pet fish' problem (which is the bane of prototype accounts of content) disappears; since extensions compose, the extension of 'pet fish' is just what it should be: all and only things that are both pets and fish are in the extension of 'pet fish'.

And, anyhow, reference must be all that there is to content, since reference is the only semantic relation of which there is a prayer that a naturalistic account will be forthcoming. The chapters that follow will provide a preliminary sketch of a kind of causal account of the reference of concepts that we think might actually work.

4 Reference within the Perceptual Circle: Experimental Evidence for Mechanisms of Perceptual Reference

Introduction

If, as we suppose, reference is a causal relation between referents-in-the-world and tokens of the symbols that refer to them—and is hence *not* to be explained in terms of intensions or their satisfaction conditions—then a theory of reference is required to provide necessary and sufficient conditions for the cause of a symbol's being tokened to be its referent. And, if the theory is to meet reasonable naturalistic constraints, its characterizations of such conditions mustn't presuppose unnaturalized semantic or intensional concepts. But there are plausible reasons to doubt that any such project can actually be carried through. It is, for example, perfectly possible for someone who lives in New Jersey in 2014 AD to refer to someone who lived in Peking in 200 BC; for example, by uttering that person's name. And it seems, to put it mildly, unobvious that a causal relation between the bearer of a name and an utterance of that name would be sufficient, or necessary, or in some cases, even possible, for the one to refer to the other.[1]

Perhaps, however, a strategy of divide and conquer might help here: first provide a theory that accounts for cases where the relevant causal relation between a symbol and its referent is relatively direct; then work outward from the core cases to ones where the relation is less direct. That is, in fact, the path we have been following; it has motivated several aspects of the discussion so far. For one: if you take reference to be a causal relation between referents and symbols, you are well advised not to take *utterances* as paradigms of symbols. There is patently nothing that it is necessary to *say* about a thing in order to refer to it. Just *thinking* about it will do; and one doesn't say (or even publish) everything that one thinks. Likewise the other way around: all utterances have causes, but merely to utter 'Sally' is not thereby to refer to everyone—or even to anyone—who is so called. This is one reason why a mentalistic version of a theory of reference is better suited for naturalization than a behavioristic one, all else being equal. *Saying* is an action; whether one says 'chair' depends on more than whether one sees a chair and knows that 'chair' refers to chairs; one might, for example, decide to keep one's chair-thought to oneself. But mentally tokening the concept CHAIR (e.g., seeing the chair *as* a chair) isn't typically a thing one *decides* to do. If, in such a case, one is attending to the chair that one sees, seeing it *as* a chair (hence tokening CHAIR) might well be a necessary consequence of having done so. Accordingly, one reason we've gone on so about *perceptual* reference—reference to things in the perceptual circle (PC)—is that if a causal theory of reference is ever to be true, the most likely candidate is the reference of a tokened mental representation to a thing that one perceives. For those cases, we think that this chapter offers a plausible first approximation, namely, that reference supervenes on a causal chain from a percept to the tokening of a Mentalese symbol by the perceiver. To that extent, we are in agreement with the empiricist tradition. From our perspective, what was wrong with Empiricism was first that it took the objects of perception to be typically mental ("bundles of sensations" or something of the sort); and second that it took the objects of thoughts, insofar as they *aren't* about things that are in the PC, to be constructions out of sensory elements. Skinner made things worse by substituting his behaviorism for the empiricist's mentalism, and his conditioning theory for their association of ideas. The first requires the tokening to be an overt response, whenever one sees a chair, and the second requires such responses to be the consequences of reinforcement. But one needn't say (or do) *anything* when one sees a chair as such; and it's far from clear what would count as doing something that might lead to reinforcement under such conditions.

By contrast, according to the empiricists, and also according to us, early stages of perceptual processing provide canonical representations of sensory properties of things-in-the-world; and a process of conceptualization then pairs such canonical sensory representations with perceptual beliefs (i.e., with beliefs of the *that's a chair* variety). The perceiver's background knowledge then mediates the inferential elaboration of his perceptual beliefs ('there's a chair, so there's something I might sit on') in ways that militate for behavioral success (though about the latter process—the interaction of perceptual beliefs with background knowledge—nothing is known that's worth reporting). This kind of theory imposes (relatively) strict limitations on the availability of previous cognitive commitments to the fixation of perceptual beliefs; the operations that perceptual mechanisms perform are more or less mandatory once a canonical sensory description of the referent is given. So the empiricists were right that there is a robust sense in which theories of perception are at the heart of theories of mind–world semantic relations;

perceptual processes are by and large 'data driven' (or, to further the computer analogy rather precisely, these processes are "interrupt driven" rather than being initiated by test operations applied to inputs—for more on this distinction, see Pylyshyn 2007, sec. 3.2.1). Causal interactions with things-in-the-world give rise to sensory representations, and sensory representation gives rise to perceptual beliefs. We emphasize, however, that this is intended as an *empirical* claim about the etiology of perceptual beliefs; in particular, it is intended to be empirical psychology rather than a priori epistemology.

We think this sort of causal sequence is sufficient to establish a reference relation between (tokenings of) mental representations and the things-in-the-world that they are mental representations of. We think that is how semantic content enters the world; it's how, in the first instance, mental representations get 'grounded' in experience. Since we're assuming that reference is the only semantic relation between symbols-in-the-mind and things-in-the-world (there is, for example, no such thing as truth in virtue of meaning) this amounts to a (very schematic, to be sure) metaphysical theory of the content of mental representations; and, since the mind–world relations that this kind of theory invokes are, by assumption, causal, the proposal is thus far compatible with the demands that we're assuming naturalism imposes on the cognitive sciences.

In short, we think the causal chains that support the reference of mental representations to things-in-the-world are of two distinguishable kinds: the first kind connects distal objects that are *within* the PC to perceptual beliefs; the second kind connects distal objects that are *outside* the PC to mental representations via causal relations of the first kind. This chapter is about the former; the next chapter is about the latter.

Perception, Attention, and Objects

Arguably the area of cognitive science that has made the most progress in recent years has been vision science (experimental and computational), which has devoted a considerable part of its energy to what is called visual focal attention.[2] In so doing, it has found itself rubbing up against the sorts of issues that we have been discussing. In particular, the goal of naturalizing reference relies on findings from the study of focal attention. Many philosophers have recognized the importance of focal attention to reference, particularly to demonstrative reference, and have suggested that to make a demonstrative reference to something in the perceived world involves attending to it. We think that something like this is on the right track and, indeed, on the track that leads to a possible way to naturalize reference. But much more needs to be said about that nature of different mechanisms involved in attention, since the intuitive sense of attention does not itself provide the essential mechanism needed for reference. Before we get to this point, we will sketch some background of the role that focal attention plays in various perceptual functions and suggest that this does not by itself give us a basis for the world–mind link that we need. The present goal is to bridge the very significant gap between what the *transducers* (or sensors, as they are referred to in psychology) provide to the *early vision system* and what, in turn, the early vision system provides to the cognitive mind. Thus, as we will see shortly, this story is committed to the view that most visual processing is carried out without input from the cognitive system, so that vision is by and large cognitively impenetrable and encapsulated in a modular architecture (Fodor 1983; Pylyshyn 1999).

Among the ways of understanding the relation between focal attention and visual reference are those that derive from different approaches to the foundations of psychology, and particularly of the study of vision: these are behaviorism, information-processing psychology, and the direct perception ideas of J. J. Gibson. These are certainly not the only possibilities. For example, there is a fair amount of current interest in what has been called "embodied vision" or "situated vision" and in motor-based vision theories (O'Regan and Noë 2002). But these can be viewed as deriving from the three foundational views just mentioned. We begin with the account of focal attention that each view has provided.

1. Attention has often been viewed as the brain's way of matching the high speed and high capacity of visual inputs from sensors with the relatively slow speed and limited capacity of subsequent visual processes and a short-term memory that receives information from the early stages. It has been likened to a spotlight that focuses limited perceptual resources at places in the visual world. There is a huge experimental literature on focal attention, and we can only touch on a very small portion of this work that is relevant as background to this chapter. We will take for granted some of the general conclusions (listed below) concerning visual focal attention, which have been drawn from many experiments.

2. Attention, like a spotlight, can be switched or moved along a (usually linear) path between visually salient objects in the field of view. This can, and often does, occur without eye movements.

3. Attention can be shifted by exogenous causes (as when it is attracted by something like a flash of light or the sudden appearance of a new object in the field of view); or it can be controlled

endogenously, as when people voluntarily move their attention in searching for some visual feature.

4. Although it seems that, under certain conditions, attention may be shifted continuously between different objects of interest,[3] the more usual pattern is for attention to switch to, and adhere to, an *object*. If the object is moving, then attention will stick to the moving object: that is, it will "track" that object. Attention is thus said to be object based. This automatic tracking of objects is one of the most consequential properties of focal attention that we will discuss in this chapter.[4]

5. The default situation is that attention tends to be unitary (hence the spotlight metaphor), although it can sometimes be broadened or narrowed (the so-called *zooming* of attention), and under some conditions it can be split into two.[5]

6. Attention is required for encoding some properties of objects in the visual field, especially for encoding conjunctions of properties.

These features of focal attention are mentioned here in order to contrast them with a mechanism that is more fundamental and more directly relevant to the theme of this book: a mechanism referred to as a *visual index* or a *FINST*.[6] FINSTs are a species of mental representations sometimes likened to such natural language demonstratives as the terms *this* or *that*, although there are significant differences between FINSTs and demonstratives. FINSTs bear a resemblance not only to demonstratives, but also to proper names, computational pointers, and deictic terms. But since all these analogies are misleading in one way or another, we will continue using the FINST neologism.

We begin by illustrating how FINSTs arose as an explanatory notion in experimental psychology. We will discuss some empirical phenomena beginning with the detection of such properties of sets of objects as the geometrical shape formed by the objects or their cardinality.

Picking Out and Binding Objects to Predicate Arguments

Determining the Numerosity and Spatial Pattern of a Set of Objects

When the cardinality of a set of individual visual objects is no more than about four, observers can report the number very rapidly and without error. Performance is not influenced by shape (except when objects form some simple familiar shape, such as a square or equilateral triangle, when enumeration is especially rapid) or color, nor by whether observers are precued as to the region where the objects will appear (Trick and Pylyshyn 1994). Although the time to enumerate a small set still increases with the number of items, the increase is very rapid (i.e., the reaction time versus number of objects graph shows an increase of only about 50 milliseconds per additional object). Enumeration of more than four items shows a different pattern; here shape, color, and location are relevant to enumeration performance. Also it takes much longer for each additional item enumerated (the RT versus number slope is greater than 100 milliseconds per item) and precuing their general location facilitates this enumeration process. The explanation we propose is that the appearance of a visual object can cause a FINST index to be grabbed. Several such indexes, up to a maximum of about four or five, may be grabbed simultaneously. Since indexes can be used to rapidly switch attention to the indexed objects, the cardinality of the set of indexed objects can then be determined by sequentially attending and counting them (or perhaps even by just counting the number of active indexes, providing these can be detected and their number does not exceed four or five). If the number of objects is greater than four or five, or if the objects cannot be individuated because they are too close together, then this method of enumeration is not available. In that case, observers must use other means to mark already counted items and to search out the yet-uncounted ones. One can imagine a variety of ways of doing this, including moving attention serially, searching for each item, or even subitizing subsets of items and then adding the results to compute the answer. These and other options for how this might be done have been proposed and tested (Mandler and Shebo 1982; Trick and Pylyshyn 1994; Watson and Humphreys 1999; Wender and Rothkegel 2000). But the relevant point here is that the quick and accurate way of doing it, by using indexes to access items in order to enumerate them, is not available unless the items are first individuated and indexed. The remaining obvious ways of counting require a serial scan, which searches for and visits each item while incrementing a counter. Thus, counting more than four items is expected to be slower (as items are located and marked in the course of being enumerated), and, unlike in subitizing, would be sensitive to the spatial distribution of items or to visually precuing their location (e.g., providing information as to which quadrant of the screen they will appear in). This is what was found (Trick and Pylyshyn 1994).

The same idea may be applied to the recognition of many simple patterns of objects. For example, Ullman (1984) examined how one might detect patterns such as Inside(x,L) or SameContour(x,y,L), where x,y, … are individual objects and L is a contour object (illustrated in figure 4.1). Whatever method the visual system uses to detect the presence of these patterns, it must first identify which individual objects the shape predicate

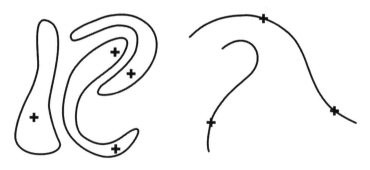

Figure 4.1

In order to evaluate the predicates Inside(x,L) or SameContour(x,y,L), which specify how the + marks are spatially related to the contours, the arguments of the predicates must be bound (or *instantiated*) to particular objects in the figure, namely the individual + marks and the contours. FINST indexes serve this external binding function.

will apply to.[7] This is where the FINST indexes come in. Once the arguments of the predicates are bound (or instantiated) to particular items using FINST indexes, the recognition process can be executed. In the case of the shape predicates examined by Ullman (1984), it turned out that the evaluation must rely on a serial processes such as "area filling," "contour tracing," or "enumeration."

The picture we are proposing is sketched in figure 4.2, which shows the FINST indexes providing a referential link from conceptual representations to distal objects. This figure does not show what the conceptual representations are like or how they use FINSTs to refer to the objects in the world. It does, however, show the conceptual representations as being organized into "object files," which play a role in allowing object properties to be represented as conjoined or as belonging to the same object. (We will return to object files later in this chapter because they play a significant role in our subsequent discussion.)

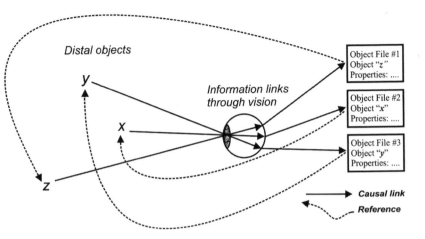

Figure 4.2
Illustration of how FINSTs work in connecting individual distal objects
with their representations. It also shows how properties and other conceptual representations may be stored or indexed in terms of the individual objects to which they refer, by using object files.

**Solving the Property Conjunction Problem (a.k.a. the "Bind-
ing Problem")**   Figure 4.2 shows that representations of (at
least some) properties of indexed objects are stored in the object
file corresponding to that object. This is not to suggest that
objects are identified by first recognizing and encoding some
of their properties. On the contrary, our view is that properties
of an object are associated with objects *after* the assignment of
indexes, if at all. Moreover, the early stages of visual processing must not conflate property tokens, thereby preventing later
stages from keeping track of which properties belong to which
individual objects. In standard treatments, in both psychology
(Treisman 1988) and philosophy (Clark 2000; Strawson 1959),
this problem is solved by encoding the *location* at which the

property tokens are detected, so that the earliest stages of vision provide information in the form: "*Property-P-at-Location-L*." But this account can't be the general case, since we can distinguish between figures even if the location of the relevant property tokens is the same in both, namely at their common center (shown in figure 4.3). There is a further problem with location-based properties, since most properties do not have punctate locations; they cover a region. Which region? Clearly it's the one that corresponds to the boundaries of the object that bears those properties. The visual system cannot apply property-at-location encoding without first identifying the object to which the properties are ascribed; so it cannot escape individuating objects *before* it decides which properties belong to which object. Berkeley was wrong to think that objects are bundles of tokens of properties; rather, as Locke thought, they are the individuals to which properties (locations included) belong. The way this is believed to work, according to Feature Integration Theory (Treisman 1988), is that in order to encode conjunctions of properties, one must first pick out the object that has the conjuncts and allocate focal attention to it in order to judge that the properties

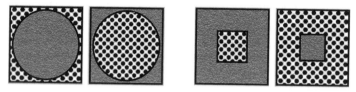

Figure 4.3
The modular "early vision" system must report information in a form that makes it possible to discriminate the two figures on the left and the two figures on the right, where both pairs are composed of identical shapes and textures, though in different combinations. To specify how it does this is to solve the binding problem.

belong to the same object; otherwise one makes frequent "conjunction errors."

The perception of a property token as a *property of an object* is extremely general. In a visual scene, properties are perceived as belonging to object tokens. In fact, when we perceive ambiguous figures, such as figure 4.4, a change in the percept is accompanied by a change in the object to which the contour is seen as belonging.

The Correspondence Problem: Keeping Track of Individual Objects Even Though (Some or All of) Their Properties Are Changing

Visual representations must be constructed dynamically. Each second of our waking life our eyes are moving very rapidly in movements called *saccades*, during which they can reach up to 900 degrees per second, and they are blind to any pattern they move over. Between successive saccades they rest only briefly in what are called *fixations*. Visual representations must be constructed over a series of such eye fixations. There is also evidence that visual representations are constructed over time even *within* individual eye fixations.[8] In addition, the objects we perceive typically change location as they move relative to the observer and the larger space, which in turn results in changes in illumination. In each case, the problem arises of establishing a correspondence between objects identified at different times, so that they are seen as the same object, as opposed to being seen as a different object when their properties change. One way this could be done is by encoding each object at time t_1 in terms of a rich enough set of properties so that they would uniquely identify the same object at time t_2. But this is unlikely, even if such

Figure 4.4

The "Rubin's vase" formed by two profiles is an ambiguous figure that appears to change from being seen as a vase to being seen as two profiles. As the percept changes, the contour changes from belonging to the vases to belonging to the profiles. This sort of "belonging" is computed early in the visual process.

properties could be found, for several reasons. One is that the solution to this correspondence problem must work even when all the objects have identical features and differ only in their histories—they count as different individuals because they came from different locations or had different properties a short time earlier. Another is that the objects' properties may be changing over time (e.g., the objects might be morphing in shape as well as moving into regions with different light), so keeping track of their properties does not guarantee that they will be correctly identified as the same individual object at a later time. Even more importantly, empirical evidence shows that the visual system does not solve the correspondence problem in that way, as we will see below.

A well-known example of how the visual system computes motion from a sequence of still images is the Kinetic Depth Effect, in which dots, painted at random on the surface of a cylinder, are projected onto a two-dimensional plane. When the cylinder is rotated the dots are seen as moving in depth around the axis of the cylinder, even though of course it is obvious that they are moving on the two-dimensional plane (e.g., a video screen). To create the motion percept, individual dots must be tracked *as the same token* dots over time. In other words, a correspondence must be established between dots at each instant of time so that they can be seen as the same moving dot rather than as a sequence of different dots. What is important about this correspondence is that it depends *only* on the spatiotemporal pattern traced out by individual dots and not on any properties that these dots might have. Experiments show that such properties of a dot as its color, size, and shape do not determine the correspondence between dots over time. This finding is quite general and has been shown in a variety of apparent motion studies (Kolers and Von Grunau 1976). Shimon Ullman (1979) showed that computing three-dimensional structure from the motion of a surface depends on the latter containing discrete objects among which certain spatiotemporal relations hold, not on their properties being unchanging.[9] It appears that relations of identity and difference of moving objects depend on first deciding which parts of a display belong to the same object and then determining which objects have moved, not vice versa. The matching process for individual objects follows what are sometimes referred to as Korte's laws, which specify the optimal relations among time and distance required to establish the perception of smooth motions from a series of discrete object positions.

One of the main characteristics of visual perception that led Pylyshyn (1989, 2001) to postulate FINSTs is that vision appears not only to pick out several individual objects automatically, but also to keep track of them as they move about unpredictably by using only spatiotemporal information and ignoring visible properties of individual objects. Kahneman, Treisman, and Gibbs (1992) describe an early demonstration showing that observers keep track of individual moving objects and in so doing they also keep track of any information that they might notice about the objects (which very often includes no information at all—as shown in experiments by Scholl, Pylyshyn, and Franconer 1999a,b). As illustrated in figure 4.5, Kahneman et al. showed observers a pair of squares each containing a different letter. Then the letters disappeared and both squares moved along a roughly linear trajectory, each ending up at 90 degrees of arc from its initial position, and equidistant from where they started. At that point a letter appeared in one of the squares and the observer had to read it as quickly as possible. Kahneman et al. found that the time to read the letter was significantly faster if it appeared in the same square that it had initially been in. (The experiment controlled for such factors as the locations of endpoints, speed, and so on.) In other words, being in the same box that it started in enhances the speed of recognition of the letters, even after everything else is controlled.

Kahneman et al. explained these results by appealing to something they called an *object file*. When an object first appears in the visual field, an object file is created for it. Each file is initially empty but may be used to store information concerning the object for which it was created and with which it is

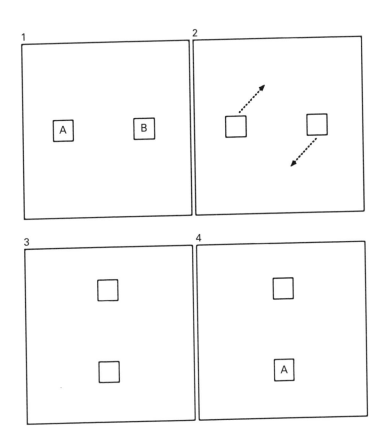

Figure 4.5

Illustration of Kahneman et al.'s (1992) demonstration that letter priming travels with the object in which the prime first appeared. Here observers see letters in boxes that then are cleared and moved to a new location. Then a letter appears in one of the boxes, either the same box it had been in or a different box. Subjects must then name the letter. When the letter reappears in the same box it is named more quickly than if it appears in the other box, even though other properties that could have favored that box (such as distance from the priming event) were controlled.

associated by a visual index or FINST. Thus there is a connection between a file and the object associated with it. The nature of connections between objects and files is, in effect, the main subject of this book.

At about the time that the Kahneman experiment was being carried out, Pylyshyn and his students demonstrated, in hundreds of experiments (described in Pylyshyn 2001, 2003b, 2007, and elsewhere), that observers could keep track of up to four or five moving objects without encoding any of their distinguishing properties (including their location and the speed or direction of their movement). These studies are germane to our current thesis, so we describe them in more detail below.

Multiple Object Tracking Experiments

An experimental paradigm ("multiple object tracking" or MOT) was inspired by the hypothesis that we can keep track of a small number of individual objects without keeping track of any of their token visual properties. Let's begin by describing this extremely simple experiment, illustrated in figure 4.6.

A few of the findings, many of which have been replicated in hundreds of experiments,[10] are as follows:

Figure 4.6

Schematic time-slice view of a trial of the multiple object tracking (MOT) task. (1) A set of objects (in this case eight circular objects) is shown. (2) Some (generally half) of the objects, referred to as "targets," are made distinct (often by flashing them on and off a few times, indicated in panel 2 for expository purposes by the halo around the targets). (3) Then all the objects move in unpredictable ways (in some cases bouncing off one another and in other cases passing over one another). (4) After a certain interval, all objects stop moving and the observer uses the computer mouse to select the subset of targets that had been identified earlier.

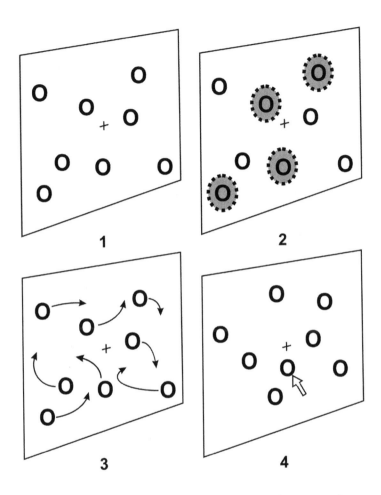

• Almost everyone (even children as young as five years of age; see Trick, Jaspers-Fayer, and Sethi 2005) is able to do this task with a display of eight objects (four targets and four nontargets; three for the five-year-olds) and an accuracy of more than 80 percent. (There are some individual differences and some effects of prolonged practice—even practice on somewhat different visual tasks, such as playing video games [Green and Bavelier 2006].)

• A number of factors affect performance, the most reliable of which is the distance between objects and the amount of time that pairs of objects remain close to one another. Other factors are in dispute. For example, it has been widely observed that speeding up the motion produces a decrement in performance (Alvarez and Franconeri 2007), but it has also been shown that this is most likely due to the confound of speed with average distance between objects. When this confound is controlled for, a number of studies have failed to show any effect of speed (Franconeri, Jonathan, and Scimeca 2010; Franconeri, Lin, Pylyshyn, Fisher, and Enns 2008).

• Many people feel that the task uses attentional resources, so that having to perform an auxiliary attention-demanding task would lower tracking performance. Yet many studies have failed to support this intuitive conclusion (Franconeri, Jonathan, and Scimeca 2010; Franconeri et al. 2008; Leonard and Pylyshyn 2003).[11] But notwithstanding such disagreements over details, it appears that tracking is both robust and limited by intrinsic properties of the cognitive architecture; in particular, keeping track of a small number of objects does not appear to exploit prior knowledge of which objects have which properties.

• In addition, tracking seems to be a primitive mechanism in the sense that it does not appear to use processes, such as extrapolation of objects' trajectories, to predict the future location of objects when they disappear from sight. When objects disappear briefly, either by being extinguished on the video display or by passing behind an opaque screen, tracking performance is typically not impaired (Scholl and Pylyshyn 1999). With slightly longer gaps, performance is best when objects reappear exactly where they had disappeared, as opposed to where they would have been had they kept moving in a straight line while invisible

(Keane and Pylyshyn 2006). This suggests that there is local spatial memory but no prediction of future location. Direct study of the effect of change of direction during gaps in visibility shows that when objects reappear having suddenly changed direction by up to 60 degrees, tracking is not impaired (Franconeri, Pylyshyn, and Scholl 2012).

• Distinctive properties of objects do not appear to help in tracking them. Indeed, observers do not even notice when objects disappear and then reappear a short time later having changed their color or shape (Scholl, Pylyshyn, and Franconeri 1999a,b). Researchers have also examined the effect on tracking when the color or shape of objects changed, either suddenly while objects are invisible (due to being behind an occluding surface or when all objects disappear briefly) or more gradually during a trial. Tracking when no two objects have the same property at any given time (their properties changed asynchronously) was compared with tracking when all objects have the same property at a given time (their properties changed synchronously). When the motion algorithm kept objects from hitting or intersecting one another (e.g., they bounced off an invisible "fence" around the objects, or the objects were kept apart using an inverse square repulsion method), no difference was observed in tracking between the all-objects-same and no-objects-same conditions (Dennis and Pylyshyn 2002). This shows that relations among object properties is not used to enhance tracking except perhaps in distinguishing objects that are very close together.

In all the studies described so far, the targets are indicated by flashing (or blinking) them briefly before the object movement (the actual tracking task) begins. Flashing is a property that can be rapidly and accurately detected in search tasks and is minimally sensitive to the number of nontargets in the task. This sort of property is often said to cause "pop out" in search tasks. In our MOT task, this type of property is likely to capture or "grab" visual indexes. But what about properties that can clearly differentiate targets from nontargets but do not pop out (such as certain color differences)? These sorts of properties do not, for example, allow the segregation of different regions. In figure 4.7, the panel on the left shows that one can easily visually distinguish the pattern formed by the small squares; but in the panel on the right it takes focal attention to pick out the boundaries of the pattern. The circle–square distinction yields pop-out discrimination while the circle with diagonals at different angles does not, even though both can easily be distinguished if we focus attention on them.

Yet it seems that we can pick out a subset of objects to be tracked, even if the difference between targets and nontargets is *not* a pop-out feature. We can, for example, decide to track the red

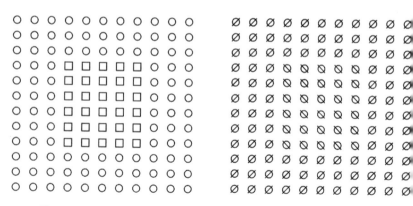

Figure 4.7
Objects with clearly distinguishable properties may nonetheless differ in how readily and automatically they cluster and how potent they are in grabbing FINST indexes.

objects and ignore the blue ones, or to track the square objects and ignore the round ones (as in figure 4.7). In several experiments (described in Pylyshyn and Annan 2006), we showed that observers can indeed select targets in a MOT task on the basis of non-pop-out features, even under the extreme conditions when the targets are the ones that did not blink (while the nontargets blinked). But to do so, observers require more time to examine the initial cue display containing both types of objects. Moreover, the more targets that must be distinguished in this way, the longer observers need to examine the cue displays. This was interpreted as suggesting that in cases where features are indexed ("FINSTed") under voluntary control, the process requires using focal attention to search the visual scene serially, looking for particular task-relevant features. As each of these objects is found by focal attention, it enables the automatic index-grabbing and tracking processes to run their course. So the suggestion is that, in the case of task-relevant properties, focal attention acts as a preparatory enabling mechanism for a basically reflexive "grabbing" operation. Or, to put the same claim in other terms, the empirical results so far suggest that the early processes of visual object tracking are "modular": bottom up, encapsulated, and object based, rather than dependent on the recognition of specific properties. Which properties cause indexes to be grabbed is determined by the architecture of the early vision system, which also determines whether or not any of these properties are encoded (including, in particular, the property of being located at a particular place in some larger frame of reference[12]). The earliest perceptual operation closely resembles the function carried out by natural language demonstratives, such as the words *this* or *that*: they pick out but do not describe individual perceptual objects. Computer pointers do the same in data structures, notwithstanding the fact that they are called "pointers," which misleadingly suggests that they pick out objects by their location. The "locations" in a computer system are only abstractly related to physical places.[13]

The existence of an encapsulated stage in visual processing is important to the story we have been telling, because if there is to be a naturalized account of reference it will have to begin where patterns of light first come in contact with the visual system. Moreover, at this stage, the process will have to be characterized without reference to conceptualized information, such as propositional knowledge. On pain of circularity, conceptual knowledge has to make contact at some stage with causal and nonintensional properties of the world. According to the view we have been developing, what happens at this stage begins with objects grabbing FINST indexes and ends with a description of the input in terms of a subset of the conceptual categories (viz., the categories relating to the visual appearance of objects). This process does not use conceptual knowledge from long-term memory, although it very probably uses a nonconceptual memory internal to the module itself inasmuch as there is clear evidence of top-down effects *within* the visual system (e.g., most Gestalt, "amodal," or Kanizsa completion effects, as well as perceptual constancies).

It may seem counterintuitive that early vision does not use information from memory about such things as the likelihood that the particular object token currently indexed is a member of a particular kind. For example, the visual system often seems to use information about the world at large in computing the three-dimensional form of particular objects from the two-dimensional proximal pattern on its retina (Pylyshyn 1999). To understand this apparent inconsistency, we need to distinguish between general, more or less permanent information—which may plausibly be built in to the architecture of the visual system—and information about particular objects or object kinds. David Marr was arguably the person most responsible for making that distinction, although in somewhat different terms from those we use here. His claim was that evolutionary pressure resulted in certain constraints on interpretation being "wired in" to the visual system. He called these "natural constraints"; researchers after him have been able to uncover many such constraints (see, e.g., Brown 1984; Dawson and Pylyshyn 1988; Hoffman 1998; Pylyshyn 2003b; Richards 1988; Ullman 1979). This is similar to the claim that infants are constrained in the grammatical structures they can learn by virtue of the natural constraints embodied in their language module and described by Universal Grammar.

For example, the apparent motion produced by putting objects in one temporal frame in correspondence with objects in a second temporal frame could be explained in several ways, including the application of simple heuristics.[14] Take the example illustrated in figure 4.8. When the top pattern is repeatedly followed by the bottom pattern, what is seen is apparent motion of the group of dots. Which particular motion is perceived depends on which objects in the first (top) figure are seen to correspond to which objects in the second (bottom) figure. This example of the visual solution of a correspondence problem reveals a property of the visual architecture and also the operation of a natural constraint. Intuition might suggest that the simplest correspondence would be based on the closest neighbor or on a linear translation that would yield the motion shown in panel A. But now suppose the second (bottom) pattern is rotated as in panel B. There are several possible sets of correspondences, including one linear translation and two different rotations. What is seen, however, is a square pattern of objects moving and also rotating counterclockwise from the first pattern into the second. The principle that we proposed to explain this derives from the fact that, in our world, punctate features tend to arise mostly from discontinuities on the surface of rigid objects. If the visual system had internalized this natural constraint, it would solve the correspondence problem by pairing not just the nearest items, but the pattern consistent with the four items being on a rigid surface and then choosing the minimum rotation. This leads to a solution shown in figure 4.8B, where the nearest neighbor condition is modulated by the rigidity constraint (Dawson and Pylyshyn 1988). Many such solutions of perceptual problems can be traced to general properties of the world that the organism lives in. But what happens if there is object-specific information concerning the identity of the objects? For example, suppose the objects differ in shape, color, or texture, as in panel C—does the similarity of objects override the simple rigidity constraint? The answer is: it does not. The spatiotemporal constraints override the color or shape continuity, thus demonstrating the primacy of these constraints.

Later we will show cases where spatiotemporal constraints override not only such properties as color and texture, but even very strong and intuitively salient principles of physics, such as the impenetrability of solids.

Since everything that happens in a creature's environment conforms to laws of nature, one might well wonder which environmental regularities come to be mirrored by properties of perceptual architecture and which do not. Given the empiricist tradition that has colored the past half-century of psychology and biology, one might expect the most frequent or perhaps

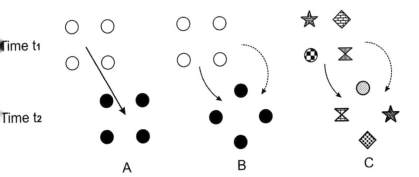

Figure 4.8
This shows how the correspondence problem is solved in a particular case. The two figures on the left illustrate that there is more to establishing correspondence than linking "nearest neighbors," and the figure on the right shows that the correspondence is solved without reference to the properties of the objects themselves (Dawson and Pylyshyn 1988).

even the most important regularities to be integrated into the architecture of the organism. But it turns out that the constraints embodied in the architecture of vision tend not to be the ones that are most frequently encountered. The visual constraints that have been discovered so far are based almost entirely on principles that derive from laws of optics and/or projective geometry. Properties such as the occlusion of relatively distant surfaces by opaque surfaces closer to the viewer are among the most prominent of these principles, as are principles attributable to the reflectance, opacity, and rigidity of bodies. However, other properties of our world—about which our intuitions are equally strong—do not appear to have a special status in the early vision system. In particular, the perceptual conflict is rarely resolved so as to respect such physical principles as that solid objects do not pass through one another. Consequently, some percepts constructed by the visual system fail a simple test of rationality or coherence with certain basic facts about the world known to every observer. Apparently, which features of the world are architecturally represented can't be explained by appeal to merely statistical regularities in the environment.

Take the example of the Pulfrich double pendulum illusion (as described by Leslie 1988). Two solid pendulums, constructed from sand-filled detergent bottles, are suspended by rigid metal rods and swing in opposite phase. When viewed with a neutral density filter over one eye (which results in slower visual processing in that eye), both pendulums are seen as swinging in an elliptical path, but with one seen as following behind the other (this manipulation results in the phase between the two pendulums being between 0 and 180 degrees). As a result of these differences in their perceived trajectories, the rigid rods are seen as passing through one another even though they are also seen to be solid and rigid. In such cases, "impossible" interpenetrations of solid objects do not seem to be blocked by the visual system, even though they are clearly at variance with what we know about how things happen in the physical world. Other examples of this same violation of solidity are well known to vision science. For example, when a trapezoidal window is rotated about a vertical axis, it is seen not as rotating but as oscillating back and forth. Yet when a rod is attached to the axis so it rotates with the window, it is seen as rotating while the rigidly attached window is seen as only oscillating. Consequently, at certain points in the rotation the rod is seen as penetrating the solid window frame (this and other such examples are discussed in Rock 1983).

Another well-known example is the famous Ames room, a distorted room with no actual rectangular surfaces, constructed in such a way that the projection of every line and polygon in the

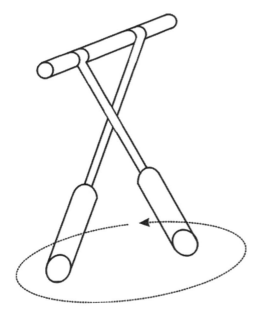

Figure 4.9
The Pulfrich double pendulum. The two pendulums swing out of phase side by side, with one swinging left while the other is swinging right. When viewed binocularly, with one eye looking through a neutral density (gray) filter, they both appear to swing in ellipses. The result is that the pendulums are seen as passing through one another. This and many other examples show that vision does not incorporate even physical constraints as obvious as the impenetrability of solid objects.

room onto the retina of an observer looking through a peephole is identical to the projection that would arise from an actual three-dimensional room with walls at right angles to each other and to the floor and ceiling. (The reason it is possible to build such a room is that there are many ways to build a three-dimensional object that projects onto a given two-dimensional pattern—the 3D-to-2D mapping is many-to-one.) But if someone walks from one side of this room to another, the observer at the peephole sees that person enlarge and shrink as she appears in different parts of the room. This happens because the different parts of the room are higher or lower, but in such a way that all the edges and two-dimensional figures (including walls and windows) appear to be rectilinear when viewed from the fixed point (several full-sized Ames rooms have been built, including one on view at the San Francisco Exploratorium, shown in pictures in Pylyshyn 2003b).

To summarize the moral of this section: many cases in which our visual system provides unambiguous (and usually veridical) percepts, despite the inherent ambiguity of the two-dimensional image, can be explained without having to assume that the visual system draws inferences from specific knowledge regarding what a particular three-dimensional scene is likely to contain. Although the *beliefs* we come to have about what is in the scene invariably take into account what we know, the output of the early vision system, or to put it loosely (though we believe correctly) *the way particular things look*, does not take such knowledge into account. The visual system is so constructed, presumably because it has become tuned over eons of evolutionary history so that the interpretations it is able to make are severely restricted. This range of alternatives is specified by principles (or "rules") such as those discussed by Hoffman (1998), Marr (1982), and Richards (1980), which can be understood as limitations of the possible interpretations that our visual system is capable of making. This is very similar to the case of language acquisition, where Universal Grammar can be seen as expressing the limitation in the structural inferences (grammatical analyses) possible in the normal acquisition of a language (so, for example, certain types of languages cannot be acquired by humans through the usual means used by young children, who merely hear the language and are not taught it by being exposed, among other examples, to instances that are identified as being unacceptable utterances of the language). In the case of vision, the structural limitations (or the natural constraints) are invariably associated with spatiotemporal and optical properties. Consequently, they do not reflect high-frequency properties of the world so much as those critical properties that animals need to keep track of in order to survive as mobile agents. The question remains why some such reliable environmental regularities come to be instantiated in the perceptual architecture while others do not. The probability that one rigid object in a creature's environment will pass through another is zero; but the architecture of the visual system appears *not* to be constructed to reject perceptual interpretations in which they do. No merely evolutionary explanation (e.g., an increased probability of contribution to the gene pool) can account for such facts; a creature that persists in trying to walk through solid objects is unlikely to contribute much to the local gene pool.[15]

Objects and Encapsulation

The empirical evidence we have reviewed suggests that initial contact between the world and its perceptual representation begins with only a highly restricted sample of the objects and states of affairs being represented. A plausible first approximation suggests that percepts are initially represented as "indexed objects" or as "this" or "that." Evidence suggests that the first stage in building perceptual representations is the individuation and indexing of objects. The very process of indexing objects requires that they can generally be tracked as they move or change their properties: they are picked out and tracked as individual objects. Indeed, we strongly suspect that what we have been calling "objects" *just are* things that can be tracked. Accordingly, since tracking is a reflex, which is to say that it doesn't involve the application of any concept, the concept OBJECT need not come into the process of visual perception *at all*. That's just as well, since, so far at least, no one has been able to provide a plausible account of what the concept OBJECT is.[16]

The perceptual system indexes and tracks objects not by picking out things that fit certain descriptions ('physical', or 'follows a smooth trajectory', or some such), but rather via a world-to-mind causal link. Certain things in the perceptual world happen to grab indexes and can then be tracked as they change properties and locations. It is this primitive tracking process that determines that they are the same objects when they change their locations in a quasi-continuous motion.[17] Thus our treatment of the early stages in perception has turned on the notions of *object* and of *tracking*, both of which are causal world-to-mind processes, and neither of which need involve conceptualization.

It goes without saying that the picture is incomplete in many ways, including the questions of how information other than what is contained in object files is assimilated into cognition and of how one can represent relational properties among several percepts or referents that are not currently visible. More on such matters in chapter 5. There is, in any event, increasing evidence over the last decade that the amount of visual information that is made available to cognitive processes by visual perception per se is much less than has often been supposed. The phenomenology of vision suggests that visual perception computes a finely detailed and panoramic display of dynamic information that the environment provides, whereas there is now considerable evidence that nothing like this quantity and quality of information is passed on from early vision to the cognitive mind. None of the assumptions introduced so far speak to the question of whether large amounts of information may be stored very briefly in some sort of "iconic" form prior to FINST-ing and other perceptual processes that early vision performs. These and many other such questions await further empirical study. But we do believe that the information channel from the eye to visual cognition (in particular, from the eye to the fixation of perceptual beliefs—e.g., *this is a chair*; *that is a pineapple*; and so forth) is much more limited than has widely been believed. The evidence that this is so comes from experiments and from clinical observations that show various sorts of shortcomings of vision in relation to an assumed wide bandwidth of the visual sense. There are, for example, various limits or "blindness" in the visual modality, including:

• *change blindness*, in which, despite a rich phenomenology, people are unable to report major changes in a scene that occur during a brief disruptive gap caused by a saccade or by presentation of a series of images varying in some major content;

• *inattentional blindness*, in which people fail to notice a task-irrelevant stimulus feature that occurs when they are attending to something else—even when they are looking directly at the critical feature;

• *repetition blindness*, in which, when patterns are presented in rapid serial streams, many of the items are not recalled, even when they are presented twice (Kanwisher 1991); and

• various sorts of brain damage symptoms, including:

  ◦ *blindsight*, in which patients with lesions in their primary visual cortex are unable to report things in a "blind" part of their visual field and yet can react to them nonverbally (e.g., by pointing); and

∘ *visual agnosia*, especially in cases where patients who are unable to recognize familiar patterns (e.g., faces) are still able to carry out accurate motor actions such as reaching and grasping and moving around. Examples include the celebrated case of DF discussed by Milner and Goodale (1995) and a case described by Humphreys and Riddoch (1987), both of which show that the phenomenology of seeing and the ability to make certain recognition-responses are distinct from the ability to navigate without bumping into obstacles and even the ability to reach for objects with motions that in minute detail are like those of people with normal vision.

There are many other differences between how the visual world appears in one's conscious experience and the information (or lack of information) that can be demonstrated in controlled experiments. For example, as far back as 1960 it was shown that information available from brief displays is neither the small amount demonstrated by experiments in reading or searching nor as encompassing as one's phenomenology suggests (i.e., that we have a panoramic picture-like display of finely detailed information). What we do have is partially analyzed information that is highly incomplete and that must be scanned serially in certain restricted ways. For example, the well-known "visual icon" that Sperling (1967) demonstrated using a method of partial report suggested that this sort of information decayed in about a quarter of a second, but he also posited a form of representation between vision and response which he characterized as a serial process that prepares a "motor program" in advance of making the response and that takes considerably longer than a quarter of a second. O'Regan (1992) also made a strong case for the poverty of functional information in relation to visual phenomenology.

It's important to bear in mind that encapsulation of a mental mechanism can work differently for different topics; it might be encapsulated with respect to some kinds of information but not others, or with respect to some of its functions but not others. A great deal of research on perceptual-motor coordination (mentioned above) has shown that some visual information is unavailable for recognition and for conscious description but may play an important role in motor control. Some patients who had severe visual agnosia (so much so that they could not visually recognize their partners) nevertheless could navigate their way and could reach around obstacles to grasp some item of interest (Milner and Goodale 1995). In the present case, we need to ask whether there are considerations other than phenomenology for believing that more information is available to cognition than is encoded in object files (which is, we're assuming, largely about the appearance-determining properties of the object that grabbed a particular FINST). The assumption of object files was, after all, initially motivated largely by considerations about the binding problem (or the conjunction problem), which is needed to explain how we can distinguish between two stimuli that have the same collection of properties in different combinations (e.g., how a red square next to a green triangle is distinguished from a green square next to a red triangle). The suggestion that perceived properties are bound to FINSTed objects (rather than the other way around—that objects are constructed from the prior perception of properties) has greatly illuminated such matters.

Our current guess is that information available in the early vision module is largely concerned with the shapes of objects. But the idea that there are knowledge-independent shape representations suitable for use in category recognition—say, by looking in a form-to-category dictionary—is well known in computer vision. A great deal of work has gone into the development of computer methods for deriving object categories from shape categories, including the use of generalized cylinders or cones (see figure 4.10), deformable mathematically characterized surfaces, structural decompositions (Pentland 1987), Fourier methods, and many other mathematical techniques. In short, various approaches to shape-based categorization of visual objects are available from research on computer vision. Some of them, mentioned above, attempt to fit what might be thought of as a rubberized surface (think of a net or soap bubble) to the outside of the object. The aim is to create general deformable models to both efficiently encode a scene and capture similarities between scenes. The techniques provide a mathematical surface deformed to encapsulate the shape of the scene so that salient aspects (e.g., location of types of maxima, minima, and inflections) are represented by mathematical parameters that carry rich information allowing subsequent identification of the scene.

Another approach, proposed by many researchers in both computational vision and human vision, relies on part-decomposition as a step toward canonical descriptions of objects (Biederman 1987; Marr and Nishihara 1987). The standard reusable parts (referred to as *geons*) are identified by a technique not unlike parsing a sentence into constituents and syntactical relations among them. An example of the decomposition of a human shape, with each part represented by generalized cylinders (or cones), is shown in figure 4.10. The use of some standard form of object-part representation, such as provided by geons, allows an object to be represented in an economical manner: cylinders have as few as seven degrees of freedom (diameter, length, orientation

Figure 4.10
Illustration of generalized cones and polygons used as the basis for representing arbitrary shapes. Primitives used in constructing canonical shapes are called *geons* (Biederman 1987).

in three dimensions, and location of the origin at one end of the cylinder). These individual components may be hinged together, so their relative orientation is parametrically encoded.

A number of experiments showing that people's ability to recognize objects under conditions of rapid presentation, as well as the errors they commit in generalizing them to similar objects, can be explained by assuming a representation that decomposes the objects into components (Biederman 1987, 1995). Pairs of objects with similar components and relations are perceptually similar. In addition, various other findings fall nicely into this picture. For example, pairs of figures were presented in a memory or identification experiment where parts of the figures were deleted. When the deleted part corresponded to a geon it was more often misrecognized even though the amount of line segment erased was the same as in the control pairs. Recognition of objects under degraded perception conditions was improved when the objects were primed immediately before presentation by a brief display of the parts and their relations. These and many other experiments suggest that subjects analyze objects into component parts and relations in the course of recognizing them as tokens of familiar objects.

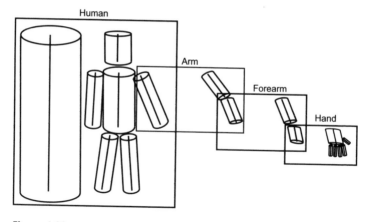

Figure 4.11

A sketch of a representation within a modular vision system that shows the decomposition of a shape into parts each represented by generalized cylinders. Such a system may use FINST indexes to keep track of the parts (from Marr and Nishihara 1978).

One might wonder why we have placed so much emphasis on shape, as opposed to other properties of indexed objects. We've done so because empirical data suggest that shape is perhaps the most salient perceptual property that distinguishes objects visually. It is also one of the central perceptual properties in virtue of which objects are seen as belonging to the same *basic category* (to use the term introduced by Rosch, Mervis, Gray, Johnson, and Boyes-Braem 1976), and objects with the same shape tend to have other properties in common as well (see also the review in Mervis and Rosch 1981). It is also a property that can be represented in a constructive manner, since it lends itself to a hierarchical structure (as shown in figure 4.11). Shape also tends to be invariant under many transformations such as translation, scaling, light conditions, and direction of view.[18] Because of its importance for the type-classification of objects, shape has been studied extensively in computational vision, where methods of encoding have been developed.

Some conditions must be met by the modular system we envision.[19] We have already introduced the idea of a canonical representation of shape, which we will denote $\mathfrak{L}(x)$. The visual system might map the shape of the object before it onto a canonical form and then may look up this shape in a shape-table and "recognize" it—that is, propose a conceptually described (perhaps familiar) object that might fit the form. In order to compute the equivalence class $\mathfrak{L}(x)$, the early vision module must possess enough machinery to map a token object onto that equivalence class using only sensory information and module-internal processes and representations, without appealing to general knowledge. The module must also have a small number (perhaps four to five) object files, because it needs those to solve the binding problem as well as to bind predicate arguments to objects. FINST indexes are also essential for using the recognition-by-parts method to recognize complex objects (as described in Biederman 1987) since that requires keeping track of token object-parts. Processes inside the visual module would allow it to look up a particular shape type $\mathfrak{L}(x)$ in a catalog of shape types. Yet this machinery is also barred from accessing cognitive memories; thus it could not carry out general inference processes.[20]

The idea of a canonical form $\mathfrak{L}(x)$ has seen considerable work in computational vision. It is a rather more complex idea than we have suggested so far. First of all, the canonical form is not a fully specified three-dimensional shape. Because it represents an equivalence class of object shapes, many detailed properties are omitted in the many–one mapping from token object to canonical form. The canonical representation may also embody a set of related viewpoints, so $\mathfrak{L}(x)$ may consist of a set of what are called *aspects* of the shape. More generally, a shape representation may consist of a set of aspects that form a topological structure (called an *aspect graph*) of the edges, junctions, and other discontinuities seen from a series of viewpoints. As the viewpoint changes gradually, such a representation will remain fixed until, at some critical viewpoint, additional discontinuities come into view and existing ones become occluded by parts of the object. Thus an aspect graph is a graph of potential aspects that capture the canonical form of an object. These have been studied mathematically in detail by Koenderink (1990a,b). David Marr used the term "2½-D sketch" to denote a representation that embodies both an orthographic (pictorial) and partial depth information. We may view our canonical form as an aspect graph or a 2½-D sketch. As noted above, it is also closely related to the *basic category* described by Mervis and Rosch (1981) and Rosch et al. (1976), which plays an important role in recognition and memory.

So we come to a highly provisional picture of how the causal relations between world and mental representations as well as causal relations *among mental representations* might play a role in early vision (illustrated in figure 4.12). Like many other semantic referentialists, we hold that the content of a creature's mental states supervenes on causal chains between those states and things-in-the-world. But, unlike referentialists who are also behaviorists, we assume that such causal chains have quite often themselves got mental states among their links; and unlike the British empiricists, we think that causal relations between mental states are typically computational rather than associative.

We want to emphasize the distinction between two sorts of claims that figure 4.12 is intended to illustrate: the first is that there are reasonably plausible ways in which computational perceptual processes might support causal relations between

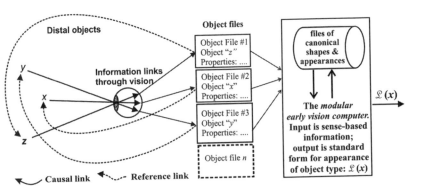

Figure 4.12
The FINST model of the modular vision system augmented to compute canonical equivalence classes of objects' sensory-based appearance. Other links (not shown) might allow for the possibility that focal attention could scan distal objects for the presence of other indexable objects meeting some general criterion (e.g., being to the left of a particular indexed object).

things-in-the-world and the fixation of perceptual beliefs. We think this provides an essential first step toward the naturalization of reference; chapter 5 hopes to carry the naturalization process further. The second claim is that this sort of model is compatible with data suggesting that many such processes are more or less encapsulated from cognition at large; perception is one thing, thought is another, "New Look" theorists to the contrary notwithstanding (Fodor 1983; Fodor and Pylyshyn 1981; Pylyshyn 1999). We're aware that these two claims are independent in principle, but, as things now stand, we're prepared to bet on both.

The Takeaway

If reference is a relation between a (mental) representation and a thing-in-the-world, then semantic theory is faced with the question what this relation could consist in. And, if naturalism is a ground rule, the answer it gives must be some or other variant on the notion of a causal connection or hook-up. But what kind of causal hook-up could that be? Notice that, though they are certainly related, this "mind–world" problem is *not* the traditional mind–body problem. Suppose, for example, it turns out that mental states really are neural states (whatever, exactly, that means). So we can all sleep safe in our beds; the traditional mind–body problem is solved; dualism is false; beliefs, desires, and the like are just brain states. Still, the question persists: How do these brain states manage to be *about things-in-the-world*? How could they have *semantic contents*? How could they refer to things? Short of answering such questions, neurological monism doesn't give us propositional attitude realism or representational realism more generally. And we need propositional attitude or representational realism, because all the serious cognitive science we've got takes for granted that an organism's behavior is (very often) caused by interactions among its representations and by interactions between its representational contents and things-in-the-world.

Our working assumption in this book is that semantic relations between the mind and the world are "grounded in" causal relations between the mind and things in the mind's perceptual circle. This isn't, of course, to say that all you can think about is the things that you can see. But it does claim that *the mental representation of things that aren't in the perceptual circle depends on the mental representation of things that are*. Very roughly, it depends on reference-making causal chains that run from things you can see (or hear, or touch, or smell, or otherwise sense) to mental representations of things outside the PC. In effect, reference in thought depends on perceptual reference, which in turn depends on sensory transduction; and at each step, it's causation that provides the glue.

Some very sketchy suggestions about how minds can think about (hence refer to) things that aren't in the PC will be the topic of chapter 5. Patently (and empiricists to the contrary notwithstanding) minds do think about things outside their PCs quite a lot of the time: for example, they remember things, imagine things, infer things, predict things, hope for things, dread things; and so forth, on and on. And the things that minds remember, infer, hope for, dread, and so on aren't, in any serious sense, "constructions" (logical or associative) out of sensations. This chapter, however, has been occupied solely with *perceptual* reference, that is, with reference-making causal chains that run from things in the PC to mental representations of such things in the head of the perceiver, typically via the detection of sensory properties. It's just a truism that you can only perceive things that are in your the perceptual circle.

We've been making suggestions about kinds of psychological mechanisms that might underwrite this truism. Some of our suggestions have appealed to methodological or metaphysical assumptions (naturalism requires mental processes to be causal); some of them appeal to what seems, so far, to be the drift of empirical findings (perceptual processes are, to a surprising extent, encapsulated from the perceiver's background of prior cognitive commitments; the basic mind–world semantic relation in visual perception is the demonstrative reference of FINSTs); and some of them are plausible simply for want of serious alternatives (perceptual and cognitive processes are both species of computations). This is not the sort of a priori demonstration that philosophers sometimes yearn for. But, as far as we know, it's the sort of patching-things-together by which science almost always proceeds. The next step is to think about how causal (and other) relations between things that aren't in the PC and things that are might ground the mental representation of the former.

Appendix: Gavagai Again

We've been campaigning for a semantics according to which:

1. The content of a concept is its extension; the content of CAT is the things belonging to the set of (actual or possible) cats; the content of LUNCH is the things belonging to the set of actual or possible lunches; the content of TUESDAY is the things belonging to the set of actual or possible Tuesdays; and so forth.

2. For cases that fall within the PC, the paradigm of reference is where the tokening of a symbol is caused by something that is in its extension. (What happens in cases of reference to things that aren't in the PC is the topic of chapter 5.)

But the sophisticated reader might well wonder if reference is a sufficiently strong condition on a semantics for mental representations (or, equivalently, of linguistic representations). 'Frege arguments' are usually offered as reasons for wondering that (see chapter 3); but so too are arguments for the "indeterminacy" of reference (IR) of the sort that Quine introduced in *Word and Object* (Quine 1960). And the sophisticated reader might also wonder whether, if we thought that there were sound arguments for the indeterminacy of reference, we would have to abandon the project to which this book is primarily devoted. But, for the kinds of reasons that this appendix will set out, we don't.

As with so many considerations that have importantly influenced discussions of semantics, it is less than fully clear how IR arguments should best be formulated. It is notorious that, prima facie, Quine's way of doing so depends on epistemological assumptions that maybe ought not to be taken for granted (roughly, that the data for the theorist's assignment of referents to a speaker's tokenings of referring expressions consist solely of correlations between tokenings of the expression and tokenings of things-in-the-world). This behavioristic kind of epistemology has had some rough going over the years since *Word and Object* appeared. But, we don't think that the case for IR really depends on it. For purposes of this discussion, we will consider a formulation that we think captures the spirit of Quine's indeterminacy arguments while leaving out the behaviorism.

The basic point is very straightforward: 'Cause' determines transparent contexts: if it's true that *a* caused *b*, it remains true on any substitution of a coextensive expressions for '*a*' and/or '*b*'; if it's true that yeast causes bread to rise, and that bread is what Granny eats with her butter, then it is likewise true that yeast causes what Granny eats with her butter to rise; if it's true that Paul Revere awakened our first president, then if George Washington was our first president, it is likewise true that Paul Revere awakened George Washington; and so on. But though it's quite true that there is a way of reading 'refers to' as transparent[21] that is presumably *not* the reading that referential semantics has in mind when it says that causation determines reference. What's wanted, for the purposes of a referential semantics, is something compositional, and while (the word) 'butter' refers to a substance made from milk, 'John likes to eat butter' is not semantically equivalent to 'John likes to eat a substance made from milk'. What shows this is that John might have the concept BUTTER even if he didn't have the concepts SUBSTANCE or MADE FROM (and vice versa).The long and short is: you can't individuate conceptual contents by their causes (though it's left open that maybe you can individuate concepts by their intensions, meanings, senses, or the like). To put it more in the way that Quine does: If the presentation of a rabbit in the PC causes the informant to say 'gavagai', then, presumably, the presentation of an assemblage of undetached rabbit parts does too, and vice versa. So if mental/linguistic representation requires compositionality, then the semantics of mental/linguistic representation isn't referential.

From our point of view, what's wrong with that line of argument is that we don't hold that the content of a concept is its referent; we hold that the content of a concept is its referent *together with the compositional structure of the mental representation that expresses the concept.* To put this in terms of Quine's own example, the concept PART is a constituent of the mental representation UNDETACHED RABBIT PART, but not of the mental representation RABBIT; so although the concept RABBIT is a constituent of our thought *there goes a rabbit*, the concept UNDETACHED RABBIT PART can't be. The moral: what's wrong with Frege arguments is also wrong with indeterminacy of reference arguments. Concepts can't be individuated *just* by their referents; but we never said that they could be.

In fact, there is some pretty persuasive empirical evidence that the content of the mental representation that expresses the concept RABBIT doesn't include the mental representation that expresses the concept PART (for a less abbreviated presentation of these results, see Quine 1981). Here as elsewhere, behaviorism underestimated the empirical constraints on psychological theories that experimental ingenuity may devise.

Consider a tracking experiment just like the ones described earlier in this chapter, except that the stimulus is not an array of dots but an array of dumbbells (a dumbbell is a straight rod with weights on both ends). It turns out that subjects can track dumbbells but can't track their weights (unless we remove the rod that connects them). Connecting the parts of a dumbbell creates a single new object, not just an arrangement of the parts of one (see Scholl, Pylyshyn, and Feldman 2001). Since the weights are undetached parts of a dumbbell if anything is an undetached part of anything, the conclusion is that what subjects see when they see dumbbells isn't *arrangements of undetached dumbbell parts* but, unsurprisingly, dumbbells. The world is the totality of *things*, not undetached parts of things.

This result doesn't, of course, show that the reference of 'dumbbell' is determinate, still less that it determinately refers to dumbbells. There are, after all, indefinitely many ways of specifying the extension of 'dumbbell', and it remains open that some or other of these is an ineliminable alternative to 'the members of the set of dumbbells'. (Quine mentions, for example, 'rabbit stages' and 'rabbit fusions'.) The real point is that the constraint we want to impose on a semantics for mental representations, though not intensional, is much stronger than what Quine or Frege had in mind. Identifying the content of a representation with *its referent together with its vehicle* is a way of saying that mental representations that express concepts must be compositional. We doubt very much that Quine's sort of examples show that there is residual indeterminacy when this condition is satisfied.

The reader will notice that we have carefully refrained from trying to define OBJECT or THING or the like. We don't doubt that there are such things as things and objects; but we do doubt that there are such things as definitions (see chapter 2). That said, we wouldn't be much surprised if trackability turns out to be the essence of thingness.

5   Reference beyond the Perceptual Circle

Why do we go on so about what does and doesn't happen in the perceptual circle (PC)? Not, certainly, because we think, as paradigm empiricists did, that all one's beliefs are, or reduce to, beliefs about one's sensations and perceptions. Rather, it's because we think that, if a theory of reference is to be of use to cognitive science, it must be naturalistic; and we think that if a theory of reference is to be naturalistic, it must posit a causal chain that runs from the things that thoughts are about to tokens of mental representations that refer to them; and we think that, for the case where the referent is a current object of perception, there is at least a first approximation to a story to tell about the character of such causal chains, namely, some or other variant of the one we told in chapter 4: at the early stages of perceptual processing, transductive mechanisms provide preconceptual representations of features of the light reflected from things and events in the PC. At some later stage, the perceptual system computes from such transducer outputs representations in a specialized (perhaps geometrical) vocabulary. "Basic level" representations of distal percepts are derived from these, perhaps by the application of a form-to-category dictionary ('Since it looks like this, it's probably a swan'). We aren't at all inclined to insist on the details; but, given the current drift of research in vision science, it strike us as plausible that some story along those lines might eventually be forthcoming.[1]

Complaint: "But still, everything that you've discussed so far has been about *perceptual* reference; and, surely, it is perfectly possible to refer to things that aren't currently objects of perception, hence to things that aren't 'in the PC'. So, even if, *per impossibile*, every word of chapter 4 is true, theories of referential content and theories of the fixation of perceptual beliefs are both in need of a vocabulary of mental representation that applies to things that *aren't* currently in view. For example, remote things, past things, future things, characters in novels, perfect triangles, 'theoretical entities', and so on can all be referred to and thought about, though none of them can be currently perceived, and many of them can't be perceived at all. And, perhaps worst of all, referents of concepts that weren't available to perception at one time have been known to enter the PC later on; PARAMECIUM is a paradigm case.[2] So then: What about reference *beyond* the perceptual circle? If the kind of naturalistic theory you've been pushing can't make sense of that, what good is it to psychologists (or to anyone else)?"

That is, we think, a perfectly reasonable objection; but we still aren't ashamed of endorsing a semantics that stresses the primacy of reference to things in the PC. On anybody's story, things that are in the PC have semantic properties that things that aren't in it don't; thus, only things in the PC can be referred to by *demonstratives*, which, according to us, play a vital role in the earliest stages of perceptual representation. (Since only things that are in the PC can be FINSTed, the FINST idea accords comfortably with the idea that demonstratives are a primitive kind of mental representation.) Or, for another example, and with only one kind of exception we can think of, you can't *attend to* things that aren't in the perceptual circle, though you can, of course, think about them, remember them, pine for them, and so on.[3]

We do admit, at this point, that it would be convenient to have intensions to lean on since, according to the Fregean tradition, a concept's *ex*tension contains all and only what satisfies the concept's *in*tension, so (demonstratives aside) it is not required that concepts that apply *beyond* the PC also apply *within* the PC. But if one thinks, as we certainly do, that the demands of naturalism require mental states to have causal powers (thereby excluding a semantics of senses for mental representations), what except reference is left for conceptual content to be? It's worth noting that it's not only Fregeans who have irons in this fire. If there are no intensions, that is, to be sure, an embarrassment for Frege. But likewise, what kind of content other than reference would be left to supervene on the "language-games," "rules of informal logic," "conceptual roles," and the like, of which "analytic" philosophers are so fond? What with one thing and another, a naturalistic theory of content—one that eschews intensions—had better have something to say about reference to things beyond the perceptual circle. Some hard cases follow; we're not at all sure that we've covered all such cases, but maybe these will suffice to suggest how others might be managed.

However, we want to placate the reader who complains that, in proceeding from a theory of reference that applies, in the first instance, to things in the perceptual circle, we have, in effect, fallen into a kind of recidivist Empiricism; and haven't we insisted, again and again, that Empiricism is false root and branch? Quite so, except that Empiricism was a reductive *epistemological* thesis, according to which whatever can be known about matters of fact can, in principle, be reduced to knowledge of sensations. Whereas, our view is that whatever is *outside* the PC that can be referred to must be causally connected, in one way or another, to something(s) that is *inside the PC*. We're inclined to doubt that anything of epistemological interest follows from this thesis about the roots of reference.

In fact, our inspiration is ethology, not epistemology. It is a constant refrain of the ethologists that every creature *except humans* lives in an 'umwelt' that travels with it and is bounded on all sides by what the creature's sensory mechanisms can detect. Excepting us, nobody can respond to, or refer to, or remember, or even think about, anything that isn't, or hasn't been, within its umwelt. We're exempted; we can refer to Genghis Khan (as it might be) because there is an intricate system of linguistic contrivances (not the Language of Thought but) *real* languages: English, French, Urdu, and the like) that causally connects us to conspecifics within whose PCs Genghis Khan once stood. Pace Piaget and many others, language is not what made it possible for us to think; but it is, unsurprisingly, what made it possible for us to communicate our thoughts.

We turn to treatments of several other kinds of objections that might be offered to the suggestion that all that can be referred to is what is, or has been, or will be, in the perceptual circle.

Too Far Away

Perhaps the least perplexing kind of reference to things outside the perceptual circle is to things that are currently too far away to be perceived. Surely we can refer to such things both in language and in thought? What might a naturalistic account of reference make of that?

We could try leaning on causal counterfactuals (a token of such and such a mental representation *would have been* caused by such and such if such and such *had been* in the PC); and we will indeed opt for that sort of treatment at various points in our story. But counterfactuals won't do the job here. We hold that tokenings of mental representations have the referents they do because they come at the ends of causal chains of which the referents are among the links. But it's hard to see how the mere truth of a counterfactual could cause anything. At first blush, the fact that seeing Bossie *would* cause me to believe that Bossie is a cow *if she had been here* could explain my actually believing that Bossie is a cow only if, in fact, Bossie *is* here. By assumption, Bossies that are very far away can't be current percepts; so it seems that, even if a causal theory might work for *perceptual reference*, it couldn't work for the reference of thoughts.

Would it help to give up and accept the more or less empiricist view that other-than-perceptual references to Bossie are constructs out of sensory experiences? (That wouldn't, of course, entail that Bossie herself is a "bundle of sensations"; it's presumably common ground that Bossie is protoplasm through and through.) But this only delays the problem, which reappears in respect to the reference of the sensory constituents that *non*perceptual beliefs are supposed to be constructed from. Consider, for example, my current belief that Bossie is brown; and suppose that I am not now sensing either Bossie or brownness. According to the empiricist picture, the content of my current perceptual beliefs must be constructed out of current sensations of brown. So, what about the content of my belief that Bessie is brown when she *isn't* in the PC? You can, after all, believe that Bossie is brown with your eyes closed.[4]

"Why couldn't the 'brown' constituent of my current belief that Bossie is brown be a *memory* of one of my *past* sensations of brown?" Because that too leaves us back where we started. We were worried about how, if not by satisfying an intension, anything that isn't currently being experienced could be the referent of a current token of a mental representation. Well, sensations that I only *remember* having had aren't currently being experienced; so the question now arises how *they* could be the extension of tokens of concepts like SENSATION I REMEMBER HAVING HAD. Empiricists tended to gloss over this problem because they often held that remembering a token of a past sensation involves having a token of that sensation (i.e., remembering a sensation as "replaying" the sensation). But this is no good. Remembering an agonizing pain doesn't require that you have one now.

But, so far, we aren't awfully worried. We've been imagining a program for constructing a causal theory of reference that starts with reference to things in the PC and works out from there. You might object to this that perceptual reference must be different from reference to things outside the PC because, tautologically, things outside the PC aren't percepts. But that ignores the *mobility* of one's perceptual circle; your PC follows you around as you go from place to place. That being so, you can have perceptions of brown (or of Bossie) practically whenever you wish. All you need to do is: find something brown to have a sensation of (mutatis mutandis, find Bossie and have a sensation of her).

Too Long Ago

Still, what we've said so far couldn't be the whole story about reference to things that aren't in the PC. For, even if perceptual reference is supposed to be the basic kind, we still have to worry about things that aren't in anybody's PC *now*, but once were. And, of course, my perceptual circle isn't mobile in *time* in the way that it is in *space*. At best, I can *remember* what I saw; but, *pace* Proust, I can't go back and have another look. Suppose, for example, that Mentalese contains proper names; and assume, for the sake of argument, that proper names are primitives (rather than abbreviations of descriptions). Still, though I have never seen Pericles, I can refer to him; I can think about him and talk about him. What could an intension-free semantics say about that?

Kripke tells a story about how it is possible for him, here and now, to refer to Moses: roughly, someone once baptized Moses 'Moses' (using, presumably, the Hebrew equivalent of 'Moses' to do so). In consequence, people who were present at the baptism came to use 'Moses' as Moses's name. Then people who *weren't* present at the baptism heard about it from people who were, and consequently they too came to use 'Moses' to refer to Moses. And so on, link by link, along an arbitrarily long chain that started with Moses being baptized and eventually got to Kripke's using 'Moses' to refer to Moses.

That seems entirely plausible. But Kripke apparently doesn't think that it would meet the demand for naturalization (which is, anyhow, not a project in which he seems to be much interested). His reason is that the chain of transmission that connects him to Moses starts with a baptismal *intention* (the intention that the person baptized should henceforth be called 'Moses') and, moreover, continues via the mental states (beliefs, memories, communicative intentions, and so forth) of people who came to use the name in consequence of the baptism; and, on pain of the usual problems about circularity, naturalists aren't allowed to take beliefs, memories, intentions, and the like for granted in explaining how mental or linguistic representations come to have the referents that they do.

We don't find that objection convincing. Let's assume that a causal-transmission-chain story would be a more or less correct account of how it comes about that our current utterances of 'Moses' (or thoughts about Moses) can refer to Moses. It seems to us to mistaken to argue, as we take Kripke to do, that naturalists are prohibited from telling that story about how 'Moses' got from Moses to us. It's true that, if the transmission of baptismal intentions were proposed as a metaphysical account of what *reference* is (i.e., what it is for 'Moses' to refer to Moses), then it would indeed be circular. But the story about the transmission of baptismal intentions doesn't purport to be a theory of reference in that sense; rather, it's a theory of reference *transmission*. According to our kind of naturalist, reference consists of some sort of causal relation between a representation and the thing it refers to. According to our kind of naturalist, such chains are grounded in perceptual reference. The story about the transmission of reference along a causal chain is supposed to explain how, *assuming that a reference-making mind–world connection is in place*, it can be inherited from minds to minds over time. De facto, the causal chains that connect our mental (linguistic) representations of things in the future, like mental representations of things in the past, include, in all sorts of ways, tokenings of beliefs, memories, intentions, and so on among their numerous links. But why should that perplex a naturalist? *Transmission* of reference is constituted by causal relations between people over time. But reference itself is a causal relation between mental representations and the things-in-the-world that they represent. A theory about the transmission of content can perfectly legitimately take contentful mental states for granted, even though a theory about what content *is* mustn't do so on pain of circularity.

It might be objected, even if a naturalistic account of the *transmission* of reference needn't make unexplicated appeals to intensional states and processes, still Kripke's story about how Moses came to be so called does. That's because Kripke holds that *the initial* causal link in the transmission chain—the one that initially fixes the reference of 'Moses'—is a baptism; and a baptism is ipso facto an intentional act, an act that is *intended* to be a naming. So an attempt to naturalize one of Kripke's chains of reference transmission would, of necessity, fail at the first link. But that argument too is unconvincing because, though transmission chains *can* be initiated by baptisms, they certainly don't need to be. Names can be just "picked up." Suppose that, in a fit of pique, I say to my cat, "You idiot, don't do that." And suppose that, having happened to have overheard my saying it, you should come to believe (albeit quite wrongly) that my cat's name is 'You Idiot', and hence come to so refer to him. The next link in the chain might then pick up this putative name of my cat from you, and so forth. So the practice of referring to my cat as 'You Idiot' might be initiated and maintained without anybody ever having the intention that my cat should be so called. Why, in principle, shouldn't a reference chain that started in that way lead to Kripke's using 'Moses' to refer to Moses? The long and short is that a theory about how reference is transmitted over time requires a causal chain that runs from an instance of reference fixation to an instance of reference inheritance. But, in principle at least, it doesn't matter whether any of the links in the chain are (including even the first one), so long as there actually are things-in-the-world that have the power to cause tokens of mental representations when they turn up in the PC.

Empty Concepts

We remarked in chapter 2 that the existence of "empty" but nonsynonymous concepts (concepts that are intuitively different in their semantic contents but which both have null extensions) is a prima facie argument against the view that reference is all that there is to the semantics of mental representations. If reference is all there is to content, why aren't 'griffin' and 'unicorn' synonyms? Worse still, from our point of view, empty concepts seem to favor some sort of inferential role semantics (IRS) over a purely referential one. 'Is a griffin' and 'is a unicorn' license different patterns of inference; 'unicorn' implies the creature has a horn, 'griffin' does not; maybe the intuitive difference between their contents supervenes on that. We think that there are, in fact, a number of *different kinds* of empty concepts; fictional characters work a little differently from frictionless planes, for example (see below). We will spare you any extensive enumeration; too much ado about nothing. But perhaps discussions of a few kinds of cases will persuade you that empty extensions don't make a conclusive case against referential semantics, still less a conclusive case for IRS.

A natural suggestion is that counterfactuals might take up some of the slack. There aren't any frictionless planes; but, because we know a lot about the laws of mechanics, we know a lot about how frictionless planes *would* behave if there *were* any: if a frictionless perfect sphere rolled down a frictionless inclined plane, its velocity would increase uniformly as a function of the inclination. Even though there aren't any frictionless planes or perfect spheres, *there are laws that would apply to them if there were.* Why shouldn't such laws make corresponding counterfactuals about them true? And why shouldn't such counterfactuals about unicorns be quite different from the counterfactual causal relations that griffins are in? It's true, of course, that rhetorical questions aren't arguments; but we're not, at the moment, arguing for referential semantics; we're just trying to block some prima facie embarrassing objections to it.

Reply: "It's a mistake to assimilate unicorns to frictionless planes because, though there are, as you say, arguably laws about the latter, there are none about the former. Consider, for example, 'If there were unicorns, they'd be herbivores' or even 'If there were unicorns, they'd have hearts'. Which, if either, of these is true? The only counterfactual about unicorns that we know for sure to be true is 'If there were unicorns, they would have only one horn', which is true by definition."

Fair enough; we warned you that saving referential semantics from empty extensions might require distinguishing between empty extensions of different kinds. Accordingly, our story about the semantics of 'frictionless plane' is different from our story about the semantics of 'unicorn'. Unicorns are *fictions*; frictionless planes, by contrast, are extrapolations from theories of mechanics that are independently certified. There are true counterfactuals about frictionless planes because there are laws of mechanics. There aren't any true counterfactuals about unicorns because there aren't any laws about unicorns (not even physical laws; we think 'If there were unicorns, they could run faster than light …' is neither true nor false).

Further reply: "What about square circles? It's not just that there *aren't* any; it's that there *couldn't* be any. So the extension of 'square circle' is *necessarily* empty, as is the extension of 'round triangle'. Nevertheless, the semantic content of 'square circle' is intuitively different from the semantic content of 'square triangle', which is again different from that of 'round triangle'."

We don't think this kind of consideration refutes referential semantics, but we agree that it has interesting consequences. As far as we can see, a purely referential semantics (PRS) would require *that no concept whose extension is necessarily empty can be primitive*. There couldn't, for example, be a syntactically simple mental representation that denotes all and only square circles. The reason is straightforward: as we've been describing it, PRS implies that the extension of a representation is determined *by actual or counterfactual causal interactions* between things in its extension and its tokens. But there are no possible (a fortiori, no actual) causal interactions between square circles and *anything* because 'There are no square circles' is *necessarily* true. So if there is a concept SQUARE CIRCLE (we're prepared to assume, if only for the sake of argument, that there is), and if PRS is true, then the concept SQUARE CIRCLE must be compositional, hence structurally complex, hence *not* primitive.[5]

Fictions

Maybe. But think about, say, 'Tonto' and 'The Lone Ranger' (taking both expressions to be "true" names, i.e., names rather than shorthand for descriptions). It's plausible that certain truths about the extensions of true names are analytic: it's analytic that the name 'Tonto' refers to Tonto or to no one; it's analytic that the name 'George Washington' refers to George Washington or to no one; and so on. So even if a purely referential semantics can be made to cope with all the kinds of empty-extension cases discussed so far, it can't cope with intuitions about the content of the names of fictions: if The Lone Ranger and Tonto are fictions, there aren't even any *possible* worlds in which 'The Lone Ranger' and 'Tonto' are other than coextensive (i.e., both empty). So, according to referential semantics, they are *necessarily* synonymous. IRS, by contrast, entails no such embarrassment; it can hold that your intuition that 'Tonto' and 'The Lone Ranger' aren't synonyms arises from your knowing that Tonto and The Lone Ranger *play different roles* in the familiar story. If, in short, conceptual contents supervene (not on extensions but) on conceptual roles, it's maybe[6] ok for 'The Lone Ranger' not to refer to Tonto after all.

The idea that content supervenes on inferential role has many enthusiasts, in both philosophy and cognitive science. But the more you think about it, the more it seems to beg precisely the questions that semantic theories are supposed to answer. For what's the difference between saying that Tonto and The Lone Ranger have different roles in the story and saying that *the story represents* Tonto and The Lone Ranger as different people? And if, as we rather suspect, these are just two ways of saying the same thing, then the putative example of how terms with the same (empty) extensions can nevertheless differ in content turns on a notion that is itself intensional, namely the notion of *representation in a story. Since the notion of a "role" is itself intensional, it's unsurprising, and not deeply moving, that an inferential role semantics could legitimize distinguishing between coextensive names.* Shifting the polemical turf from intuitions about meaning to intuitions about inferential roles isn't much use to a naturalist if the explication of the latter begs the case against him.[7]

Still, it should be admitted that fictional names are prima facie counterexamples to purely referential semantics. Quibbles aside, what PRS really wants to say is that *all empty concepts have the same semantic content* in any sense of semantic content that it is prepared to take seriously. And according to intuition, that's just plain false. Intuition says that 'Tonto' and 'TLR' aren't synonyms. But we think that intuition is misled in saying this. Chapter 2 suggested a way of explaining why that is: practically every term or concept comes with an aura of associations, attitudes, feelings, beliefs, quasi-beliefs, recollections, expectations, and the like. (Bertrand Russell [of all people] once held that 'or' expresses an attitude of uncertainty!) We think it's quite plausible that auras can, and often do, influence intuitions that purport to (but don't) reflect bona fide semantic truths.

Methodologically speaking, that's a good reason why cognitive scientists (linguists and philosophers very much included) should take intuitions with a grain of salt. This applies with special force to the case of characters in fiction because so much of the aura that one's concept of a character has is supplied *by the fiction*. Hamlet was chronically indecisive. How do we know? Because *Hamlet* shows us that he was. Othello was noble but a dope. How do we know this? Likewise, Iago was a plain stinker. How do we know? One of the things that authors of fiction do for a living is construct auras for an audience's concepts of their characters; and, roughly speaking, the stronger the aura, the more "lifelike" the fiction.

Shakespeare was *very* good at that. It's a middle-brow cliché that his characters seem to "step off the page." One could almost believe in Rosalind or Beatrice, if they weren't too good to be true. But (according to us) *none of that has anything to do with semantics*. What shows they don't is that, like inferential roles, auras don't support paradigm semantic properties like synonymy and modality.[8] It doesn't follow that auras can't *explain* such intuitions when they are mistaken. Intuitions are sometimes *evidence* for (against) semantic theories; but they are never *constitutive* of the truth (falsity) of semantic theories. They work much the way that observational reports do in the hard sciences; one has to take them seriously, but they're fallible.

So much for what issues nonsynonymous concepts with empty extensions do and don't raise for referential semantics. We do agree, of course, that they are prima facie counterexamples. But we don't agree that they are remotely decisive prima facie counterexamples, and we won't give up on PRS unless we're really forced to; because (we may have mentioned this before) we think that PRS is the only available candidate for a naturalistic science of cognition, and we do think that, in the cognitive sciences as in the others, naturalism is sine qua non.

Too Small

It is undeniable that some things are too small to see. And there are things that we can see now that used to be too small to see. We can now see paramecia and the like by using microscopes; and saying that we can doesn't equivocate on 'paramecium' or on 'see'. But, even back when paramecia were too small to see, they could perfectly well be referred to. Accordingly, a viable metaphysics of reference must be able to explain how they could have been referred to before they were in anyone's PC. The answer seems clear enough from the point of view of the kind of causal theory of reference that we endorse: reference requires a causal chain connecting tokens of mental representation to their referents. In paradigm cases of visual perception, one of the links in the chain is the reflection of light from a distal object onto sensory transducers that respond to them. It used to be that there were no such chains, but then Leeuwenhoek invented the microscope, and now there are. In particular we *now* can say what they *then* were referring to when they spoke of paramecia.[9]

Too Big

Is there any such thing as the universe, or is 'the universe' just a hypostatic way of saying 'the totality of things' (cf. Ryle 1949: 'the university' as a hypostatic way of saying 'all the colleges taken together')? And, if there is such a thing as the universe, is it possible to refer to it according to a causal account of reference? Presumably that would depend on whether the universe can cause anything—in particular, on whether the universe can cause tokenings of mental representations. Well, can it? We suspect that such questions are merely frivolous. But if they aren't, whose job is it to answer them? The semanticist's? The ontologist's? The physicist's? The metaphysician's? In any case, better them than us. We think a theory of reference is only obliged to cope with reasonably clear cases where a symbol refers. We'd be more than content with that.

Properties

"Abstract objects don't cause things. But we can refer to (not just instances of red but also) the color red; and to the *property of being red*; and both of these are abstract objects. So causal theories of reference must be false."

What, if anything, is wrong with that line of argument? It would be nice if there were some way around it, since, as we've several times remarked, taking conceptual content to be referential and reference to be causal promises to avoid embarrassments that intension-based theories seem unable to dodge. These include not just worries about naturalism but, as chapter 2 pointed out, by dispensing with notions like SENSE and INTENSION, referential semantics deflates Fodor's paradox, which purported to show that if concepts are individuated by senses, there can be no such thing as concept learning. This bears a little looking into.

Suppose what Fodor took for granted: if concepts are learned at all, it must by some process of hypothesis projection and confirmation (how else, after all, *could* they be learned?). It then looks as though all concepts will have to be innate. The Churchlands have suggested (Churchland and Churchland 1983) that this argument is a sort of reductio of the whole idea of a computational cognitive psychology; and even Fodor, in his darkest moments, has found it uninviting. By contrast, a referential theory of conceptual content can just shrug its shoulders. If the content of a concept is its reference, all you need to learn BACHELOR is *some way or other* of representing its extension; any mental representation that is coextensive with BACHELOR (any description that is true of all and only bachelors) will serve to do that. In particular, it's *not* required that the mental representation of bachelors that mediates the learning of BACHELOR should be a synonym of 'bachelor' since, according to a purely referential semantics, there are no such things as synonyms. It's an agreeable consequence of referentialism that it takes concept acquisition to be at least *possible*, which, arguably, sense-semantics can't do.[10]

Reference to Abstracta

We think that what makes the main trouble for a referential-causal theory of conceptual content aren't the issues about how concept learning is possible; it's how there can be reference to abstracta. In particular, since senses and the like are abstract objects, a causal-referential theory of content is sorely in need of an alternative to the thesis that "senses determine extensions." But if senses don't determine extensions, what does? We continue to hold the most promising answer to be that, in the central cases, conceptual content *is* referential, and reference *is* (or supervenes on) a causal relation between mental representations and their referents. But, since it's common ground that abstracta don't have causal powers, how could there be concepts that refer to them? How, for example, could there be concepts of redness, or of being red?

How serious is this? We think it's no worse than not hopeless. To begin with, we think that reference to a property must somehow be grounded in reference to (actual and possible) individuals that have that property. Merely possible individuals don't, of course, have causal powers any more than abstracta do. But we suppose that part of a naturalistic account of property-reference will appeal to counterfactuals of roughly the form '*if there were* an *x* that has property P, it *would* cause ...' where the *x*'s can be possible-but-nonactual. (If the naturalist we're trying to placate won't allow us counterfactuals, so be it. But we doubt that intensional psychology is the only science that this very exiguous sort of naturalism would preclude, since it is plausible that the notion of an empirical law is very much bound up with counterfactuals, and we suppose that there are [or anyhow may be] laws of cognitive psychology.[11])

Consider a kind of example that the philosopher Joe Levine is fond of. Suppose you say (or think): "I want my house to have the color of that house." This doesn't, of course, mean that I want the color to be stripped off that house and glued onto mine in the manner of frescos. What I want is that my house should be *a token of the same color type* as that house. But to what does the 'color' refer in 'token of the same color type as ...'? Plausibly, it refers to a property, namely the property of which the color of that house is an instance, and of which I want the color of my house to be likewise an instance. But, to repeat: how could an utterance (/thought) refer to a property if properties are abstracta and reference is a causal relation between representations and their referents? Properties don't have effects (though a state of affairs consisting of a property's being instantiated by an individual perfectly well can).

This distinction may strike a very hard-headed psychologist as frivolous, but it isn't. All sorts of nasty equivocations result if one fails to attend to it. Consider 'the color of Sam's house infuriates John'. Does that mean that redness infuriates John (John is red-phobic), or does it mean that it infuriates John that Sam's house instantiates redness (he doesn't care if some other houses are red, but it bothers him that Sam's is)? If you think that distinction is frivolous too, imagine that you are a developmental psychologist who is speculating on the etiology of John's pathology, or a clinical psychologist who is trying to cure him of it.

One could understand the problem "how should a purely causal theory of reference cope with reference to properties?" as raising an issue in ontology; that way of reading it would take the question to be "*what kind of thing* could properties be such that a purely referential semantics is true of terms that refer to them?" But we don't recommend that you read it that way; this ontological approach, is, we think, one of the things that makes the problem about reference to properties seem not just hard for a causal theory but hopeless on the face of it. It would, for example, be a mistake for a purely referential semanticist to ask "What sort of thing-in-the-world (or even in Plato's heaven) bears the same reference-making relation to the expression 'red' in 'red is a color' that *this apple* bears to this apple in a token of 'this apple'?" It's a mistake because, on the one hand, the semantic value of 'apple' in 'this apple' is its referent, and the content-making relation between referring expressions and their referents has to do with whether tokens of the latter cause tokens of the former; and, as we keep saying, it's a truism that properties don't have effects. So it might well seem that either causal-referential semantics isn't true or the truism is false. It appears that the cost of endorsing such a semantics is having to conclude that there isn't—couldn't be—*anything* that property terms refer to. Many a nominalist has indeed argued in more or less that way.

But this is a false dilemma. Causal-referential semantics doesn't say that there are no properties (or even that there aren't *really* any properties). Come to think of it, we're not at all clear what it would it would mean to say either of those things. Rather, purely referential semantics should say that what the concept RED contributes to the semantics of THE COLOR RED isn't its referent but its *possession condition.* In particular, to have the concept THE COLOR RED, one must have the concept that 'red' expresses in (for example) 'that red house'; roughly, it's to have a Mentalese representation type that is caused to be tokened by red things as such.

Since we are, for better or worse, already committed to a sufficient condition for having the concept that 'red' expresses in 'that red house', the semantics of 'red' in 'the color red' doesn't show that the causal-referential semantics game is over. It does, however, suggest that our "purely referential" semantics won't, after all, be *purely* referential.[12] Having the concept that 'red' refers to in 'the color red' is having a mental representation type that is caused to be tokened by (actual and possible) things that are red; so the 'red' in 'the color red' expresses a *second-order* property; it's a property that representations have in virtue of the causal properties of *other* representations; in particular, in virtue of their capacity for being caused by instances of redness. That seems reasonably natural since, from the metaphysical point of view, properties do seem to be second-order sorts of things. For there to be the property *red* is for some (actual or possible) things to be instances of redness. No doubt, if that is taken to be a *definition* of 'the property red', or as the *sense* of the corresponding concept, it would be hopelessly circular. But we don't intend any such thing; according to us, concepts don't have definitions or senses; all they have is extensions. Accordingly, all you need in order to specify the content of a concept is a description that has the same extension that the concept itself does. Having the concept of 'the color red' is having a mental representation that is caused to be tokened by actual and possible red things.

So where there has the discussion in this chapter gotten us? There are a number of prima facie reasons for thinking that a naturalistic theory of conceptual content would have to be some sort of causal theory of reference; and there are also a number of prima facie reasons for thinking that the content of one's concepts is constituted, in the first instance, by a relation between one's mind and things in one's perceptual circle; in effect, all other content-making relations are grounded in these. That may strike you as very bad news for Sherlock Holmes, Julius Caesar, merely prospective grandchildren, protons, numbers, triangles, the color red, and so on. It may thus appear that there is a large and heterogeneous collection of prima facie counterexamples to the only kind of naturalistic semantics that we've been able to think of. We would find that depressing except that that there *isn't* (actually) anybody that 'Sherlock Holmes' refers to; and, though 'Caesar' and 'proton' both have referents, we think that's compatible with a theory that says that their having referents depends on their tokens being caused, directly or indirectly, by Caesar and protons, respectively. That's just as well. Cognitive Science needs a naturalistic semantics because it needs a viable version of the representational theory of mind. It needs a viable version of the representational theory of mind because it needs a naturalistic account of the content of mental representations; and, as far as we can tell, RTM is the only serious candidate currently in view.

So here's what we take the polemical situation to be. On the one hand, it isn't disputed (except, perhaps, by philosophers attracted to a "phenomenology of the present moment," of whom there no longer are many) that theories of reference, causal or otherwise, must somehow make sense of reference to things outside the PC; and, pretty clearly, there are things outside the PC to which we can refer but to which, at best, we aren't *directly* causally connected (Julius Caesar, for example); and there are things outside the PC (properties and numbers and Sherlock Holmes, for example) that aren't causally connected to mental representations or to anything else. Taken together, however, these are an odd lot. The reason that Sherlock Holmes is outside our perceptual circle is very different from the reason that Julius Caesar is; which is again very different from the reasons that perfect triangles and the property *red* are; which are again outside the PC for different reasons than some very small things are; which is again different from the reason that our far-flung grandchildren are (to say nothing of our merely prospective great-grandchildren). Likewise, things outside our light-cones. We see no reason to doubt that (barring Sherlock Holmes and his ilk) all these things are, or could be, real. But the fact that the kinds of putative counterexamples to causal theories of reference are so strikingly heterogeneous suggests to us that perhaps they can be dealt with piecemeal. That's what this chapter has had it in mind to do.

We think that (contrary to claims that philosophers and others have made from time to time) there are no really conclusive arguments against the view that conceptual content boils down to reference; or against the view that the vehicles of conceptual content are, in the first instance, mental representations; or against the view that the reference of mental representations supervenes on their causal relations. If we thought otherwise, we would have written some other book or no book at all. Maybe, however, convincing arguments against one or another of those views will turn up tomorrow. We hope not; but if any do, we'll worry about them then. And if they don't turn up we will be much further ahead in the goal of forging a science of mind.

Notes

1 Working Assumptions

1. More precisely, reference and truth are the only semantic properties of mental or linguistic representations. But we'll have practically nothing to say about truth. We suppose that, given a satisfactory notion of reference, the notion of truth can be introduced in more or less the familiar Tarskian manner, the basic idea of which is that if the symbol 'a' refers to (the individual) *a*, and the symbol 'F' refers to (the property) F, then the expression 'a is F' is true if and only if *a* is F. There are, to be sure, lots of hard problems in this part of the woods. But we thought we'd leave them for the logicians to work out.

2. "Why are you telling me this? I am a cognitive scientist, not a metaphysician, so why should I care whether believing that John is a bachelor and believing that he is an unmarried man are the same mental state?" Well, imagine an experimental psychologist who is worried about what concepts are, some of whose subjects decline to infer from *John is a bachelor* that *John is an unmarried man* but accept the inference from *John is a teenaged auto mechanic* to *John is an unmarried man*. Do such subjects have the concept BACHELOR or don't they? In particular, do such data argue for or against the theory that concepts are stereotypes?

3. The constituents of mental representations and of propositions are concepts, and some people are squeamish about saying that concepts refer (or, for that matter, that words do). Rather, they say, referring is

what *people* do, typically by uttering linguistic expressions. Our sensibilities, however, aren't all that refined; we're quite prepared to speak either way.

4. Perhaps it goes without saying that this is all very sketchy so far; certainly nothing so far amounts to a theory of the semantics, either of propositions or of concepts, or of mental representations. At this stage, we're just setting out some of the vocabulary that we think such theories will require. But the decision to set things up this way is not mere stipulation. That sentences and propositions are both "compositional" is part of the story about why there are indefinitely many of each. Likewise, it had better turn out that the causal consequences of tokening the proposition that John loves Mary in one's head has different consequences for subsequent thoughts and actions than tokening the proposition that Mary Loves John. See practically any nineteenth-century novel.

5. Connectionists, for example, apparently want to opt simultaneously for the compositionality of mental representations and the associativity of mental processes. But they haven't, so far, been at all clear about how they might manage to do so.

2   Concepts Misconstrued

1. Visual imagery and the dual code view have received most of the attention in psychology, but other modalities of thought have also been proposed, such as kinesthetic, musical, and mathematical thinking.

2. This is not to minimize the impact that the dual code view had on psychology, since much of psychology in the 1960s and 1970s was concerned with parameters that affect learning, where "frequency of occurrence" was widely assumed to be the main factor determining both learning and recall. The advent of dual code theory opened the door to showing that properties of the *form* of representation, and not the frequency of the represented object, was the main determinant of recall. (Unfortunately the theories were built on an associative framework and it soon became clear that this mechanism was unable to meet the needs of cognitive science.)

3. We have described these few experiments extremely sketchily. Experimental psychologists carry them out in careful detail, usually with appropriate controls. But none of the details are germane to the general phenomena discussed here or to the conclusions derived from the measurements.

4. Even more puzzling is that all the empirical data of psychophysics, as well as the phenomenology of mental imagery, suggest that if images are spatial layouts in the brain, they must be a layout of patterns in three dimensions, so the display of the mental images would have to be on a three-dimensional manifold and not a two-dimensional surface, which disqualifies the visual cortex (where patterns are at best two-dimensional) as a basis for spatial properties.

5. As an example of different trade-offs, consider the expressive power versus inferential complexity trade-off discussed by Levesque and Brachman (1985), who showed that certain limited logical formalisms (which they called "vivid" representations because of their similarity to the limited expressive power of images, which do not contain quantifiers such as *all*, *some*, or *none*) can draw inferences with complexity far lower than regular inference, which runs into the infamous exponential explosion as the data-base expands. Similarly, by expressing representations in certain canonical forms it is sometimes possible to precompute a number of functions and store their values so they can then later be obtained by a "lookup table" of their arguments. In some cases this can even be done in constant time. The idea, referred to as *Memo Functions* or *Memoization* (Michie 1968), is a special case of a trade-off similar to the expressive power versus computational complexity. In this case it is referred to as the space-time trade-off, and the Memo Function idea has been used in such complex processes as top-down parsing (Johnson 1995).

6. In the philosophical literature, the sorts of points we're about to explore arose primarily in epistemology. They trace directly back to Sellars (who thought, probably wrongly, that they show that there are no "sense data") and indirectly to Kant and Frege.

7. "How can I do that?" Good question. Unlike "discursive" symbols, pictures have no way to express quantification, so they can't distinguish

'This swan is white' (or 'Lots of swans are white') from 'All swans are white'. But minds can. Ours just did.

8. The doctrine that mental representations of beliefs must have many of the properties of what is represented (e.g., orientation) caused a great deal of misdirected worry in the seventeenth century. Johannes Kepler was able to solve the problem of how light from an object is focused by the eye's lens to form an image on the retina, but he was unable to solve the problem, then taken very seriously, of how we can see an upright world when the image on the retina is upside-down (Lindberg 1976). Current worries about mental imagery suffer from a very similar mistake about mental images.

9. Of course, we don't mean that the cortex itself is two-dimensional, only that the surface of the cortex maps the two-dimensional topology of the retina. Go deeper into the cortex and you don't find a representation of the third dimension of the perceived world.

10. Leibniz's law is the principle of logic that says that if A is identical to B, then every property of B is a property of A and vice versa.

11. Perhaps you object to speaking of the 'meaning of a concept': "Concepts don't *have* meanings," you may wish to say, "concepts *are* meanings." So be it. In practice, when we wish to speak of 'conceptual content' we will usually be referring to the concept's intension or its meaning or its sense. But, since we don't believe that there actually are such things as intensions, meanings, or senses (we think that all that concepts have by way of semantic content are their extensions), our use of the other terms will be just expository.

12. See, for a classic example, Bruner, Goodnow, and Austin (1956) 1986, which is pretty explicit in endorsing a definitional theory of conceptual content. Accordingly, Bruner and colleagues test whether a subject has a concept by determining whether he is able to apply the concept correctly.

13. Though these days most cognitive scientists are dubious about it, the definitional theory of conceptual content still has many adherents among linguists; they hold that word meanings are, in many cases, defi-

nitions (which is tantamount to holding that concepts are, assuming that the meaning of a word is the concept it expresses). It is, for example, frequently claimed that there are structural (syntactical) arguments that favor a definition of 'kill' *as* CAUSE TO DIE, and likewise in the case of other "causative" verbs. There is, in linguistics, a very large literature on this; indeed, it is one of the characteristic theses of 'linguistic semantics'. But its status remains much in dispute. For what it's worth, however: '*x* killed *y*' and '*x* caused *y* to die' are clearly not synonyms; they aren't even coextensive. Because 'cause' is transitive and 'kill' isn't, you can cause someone to die without killing him (e.g., by causing someone else to kill him). See Fodor, Bever, and Garrett 1974.

14. Notice, once again, how much of the work the "etc." is doing. Perhaps that wouldn't matter if the examples really did show us "how to go on" from them; but they don't.

15. This definition of 'sensation' is, of course, blatantly epistemological; and, unsurprisingly, it begs the question why your beliefs about which sensation you are having are infallible when so many other kinds are notoriously not. By contrast, cognitive science generally prefers to talk of 'transducer outputs' rather than 'sensory experiences': roughly, transducer outputs are (directly) caused by world–mind interactions, and they (directly or otherwise) cause perceptual beliefs. We will ourselves adopt this sort of view; but, of course, it doesn't provide anything remotely like a definition of 'sensory' since nothing remotely like a definition of 'transducer' is available. And it offers no answer to even such vexed questions as what, if any, connections there are between being sensory and being conscious.

16. We think the experimental studies that Bruner, Goodnow, and Austin ([1956] 1986) take to bear on concept acquisition are really about how people acquire words for concepts they already have. In particular, they don't bear, one way or the other, on whether concepts are definitions.

17. Of course, everything belongs to more than one kind. This desk belongs to the kind 'thing in my office' and to the kind 'thing purchased at a discount' and to the kind 'wooden thing', and so forth. It is, indeed,

perfectly possible for a thing to be stereotypic of one of the kinds it belongs to but not of others. An example is given below.

18. On the other hand, there are dichotomous categories, and they do embarrass the identification of concepts with stereotypes. It is presumably a conceptual truth that there is no such thing as a number that is more or less even; but subjects will tell you that two is a better example of an even number than 78 (Gleitman 1983).

19. Assuming that stereotypes can properly be said to have extensions. It's no accident that people who hold that concepts are stereotypes are also prone to hold that the extension of a stereotype is a "fuzzy" set.

20. A general problem with the similarity space idea is that such spaces are cognitively penetrable; different dimensions (and different numbers of dimensions) are needed to characterize the same object in different contexts. Moreover, as Shepard (1964) showed, what dimensionality of space is needed depends on what aspect the observer attends to.

21. There is a variant of stereotype theory according to which there is a single similarity space, on the dimensions of which stereotypes are all located: These are said to include color, shape, sound, smell, texture, and the like—"sensory" properties (Churchland 2006). But this is just empiricism all over again unless there is a serious attempt to make clear which properties are to count as sensory (see above).

22. 'The thought that water is wet predicates wetness to water' and 'the thought that water is wet is true iff water is wet' may just well be two ways of saying the same thing. In any case, to speak of thoughts as having logical form is to invoke denotation (reference) and truth as parameters of their content. And, remember, the content of a thought is supposed to be inherited compositionally from the content of its constituents; so the fact that thoughts have logical form constrains facts about the content of concepts. All of that is overlooked if you think of the semantics of mental representations in the way empiricists and associationists practically always did; their theory was primarily a theory about the contents of *thoughts*, not about the content of concepts. We've already seen why this was so: the content of one's thoughts is constituted not only by their conceptual constituents but also by the

compositional structure of the relations of their constituents to one another. Confusing the structure of concepts with the structure of thoughts gets you into a great deal of trouble, as we are about to see.

23. "I thought you said that a mind at a given time has access to indefinitely many concepts. So how could a finite graph represent an indefinitely large conceptual repertoire?" Well, it depends on how you read 'available'. For the purpose of discussing connectionism/associationism, it's easiest to take "the conceptual repertoire available to the mind at t" to mean something like the set of concepts that are constituents of thoughts that the mind has actually tokened up to and including t. The question of how a connectionist/associationist might represent the indefinitely large set of concepts that would be constituents of thoughts if the mind could think all the thoughts that its conceptual repertoire allows for, though crucial, is generally not treated in the canonical connectionist/associationist literature.

24. The difficulty arises because matching topological networks based only their connectivity, where the relevant nodes are not independently identified first, represents an "ill-posed" problem that may not admit of a unique solution, as is the case with the problem of computing the 3D shape of an object using only its 2D projection. But, like the problem of computing a unique 3D solution, it might be solved in most cases if one constrained the possible solution space, as is done when one introduces *natural constraints* in vision (see Pylyshyn 1999; 2003, ch. 3). In the absence of node labels one might have to rely on some other means for identifying node types in order to constrain network interpretation (such as noting the connection of some nodes to sensors or to motor systems or to one of a small number of other privileged node-types). While we are not aware of any detailed proposals for how it might work in network representations, it does suggest that something of this kind should not be excluded out of hand just because matching unlabeled networks is, in general, an ill-posed problem.

25. One reason this sort of objection isn't more generally recognized is that associationists/connectionists often turn empiricist when the circularity threatens. See, e.g., Churchland 2006, who suggests, in effect, that conceptual contents reduce to connectedness in conceptual space *except*

for the content of primitive concepts, which is taken to be sensory. (See also the literature on "concept grounding," which quite often depends, in one way or other, on making the same assumption.) In this respect, much of contemporary cognitive science recapitulates Berkeley. "Those who ignore history are doomed to repeat it" includes the history of philosophy.

26. For a more extended discussion of issues raised in this section, see Fodor and Lepore 1992.

27. This appendix is a reply to Prinz and Clark 2004, which is in turn a reply to Fodor 2004.

3 Contrarian Semantics

1. We won't, however, discuss the kind of intensionalist theories that identify conceptual contents with "sets of possible worlds." That's because naturalism wants conceptual contents to affect causal powers, and we can't imagine how sets of merely possible worlds could do that. *Merely* possible things don't make anything happen.

2. It bears mention that if, as Quine argued, there is a circle of interdefinition among notions like *intension, meaning, definition*, etc., then *extension* is in that circle too. According to the usual understanding, the extension of a representation is the set of things that it applies to. But what could 'applies to' itself mean if what it means isn't something semantic?

3. We don't at all suppose that Carnap would approve of the way we use his sort of view. As we read Carnap, he was a *realist about PAs*, but he was some sort of *reductionist about PA explanations*, which he thought could be dispensed with in favor of explanations in brain science. We are *noneliminative* realists both about PAs *and* about PA explanations; in particular, we're morally certain that propositional attitude explanations don't reduce to anything that can be said in the vocabulary of brain science.

4. The reader may wish to suggest that, on closer consideration, some or all of these "alternatives" are, in fact, themselves instances of Frege-

type arguments. That may be so; for our present purposes, it doesn't matter.

5. Actually, the "inter-judge reliability" of intuitions about identity and difference of content isn't self-evident. Linguists have been at daggers drawn for years about whether or not 'John killed Bill' and 'John caused Bill to die' ('to become dead'?) are synonyms; or even whether it is possible for one to be true when the other is false (which is not, by any means, equivalent to their having the same meaning). See also the scuffle over what, if anything, the results in "experimental philosophy" show about the stability and reliability of synonymy intuitions (Fodor 2001; Carnap 1956). We don't propose to insist on this, but we think somebody probably should.

6. A similar outrage is frequently expressed when someone says that there are no such things as mental images. Of course what such a person would likely mean is that this everyday notion does not pick out a category that plays a role in explanations of the sort of thinking that goes on when a person reports 'having a mental image'. The latter phrase does point to *something* (e.g., a subjective experience), but, like "grass," it's not something that will play a role in an explanation by virtue of its phenomenal (or other everyday folk) properties. Needless to say, this requires some unpacking, which it gets in, e.g., Pylyshyn 2002, 2003a, 2007.

4   Reference within the Perceptual Circle: Experimental Evidence for Mechanisms of Perceptual Reference

1. It might be suggested—it might even be true—that a necessary condition for the *utterance* of a name to refer to its bearer is that it be caused by the speaker's intention that it do so. But it's hard to see how a parallel condition could apply to reference in *thought*s, since one doesn't usually have intentions with respect to the semantics of one's thoughts. Compare: 'From now on, when I speak about Marx I intend to be referring to Groucho, not Karl' with 'From now on, when I think about Marx, I intend to be referring to Groucho, not Karl' (Fodor 2009).

2. The term "focal attention" is used to distinguish the sort of attention that is important to us in this chapter—the relatively narrowly focused region or set of properties where visual resources are brought to bear, as opposed to more informal uses of the term as in "pay attention" or "attend to your work not to what's on TV."

3. There is even controversy as to whether the data cited in support of the view that attention must move continuously through space can be better explained by a more discrete switching of attention, together with a certain inertia inherent in the build-up and decay of attention as it recedes from the start location and builds at a goal object (Sperling and Weichselgartner 1995).

4. The claim that tracking is automatic is controversial. Anyone who has taken part in a multiple object tracking (MOT) experiment will usually report that it was not easy—that *effort* (whatever exactly that is, apart from its phenomenology) is required. To understand the claim one needs to distinguish between various senses of effort and of attention resources required by that task. Clearly one has to attend to the task and not be distracted by other activity going on in the background—it is part of the story about FINST indexes that they are automatically grabbed by certain ambient surrounding events and that some of these events can seize a FINST index currently attached to certain objects. But that is not the same as the claim that in order to track moving objects one needs to actively and perhaps voluntarily keep track of them, using a common pool of limited resources. There is evidence that secondary tasks do not as a rule cause tasks such as tracking to deteriorate (Leonard and Pylyshyn 2003; Pylyshyn 2007) unless they require selecting between competing responses (Jolicoeur 1999). Multiple object tracking also appears to be insensitive to object properties, including their color, shape, and even the speed and form of their motion (Franconeri, Pylyshyn, and Scholl 2012; Keane and Pylyshyn 2006; Pylyshyn 2009), and that the only factor that reliably causes tracked objects to be lost is proximity (crowding) among objects (Franconeri 2008, 2010), which is understandable inasmuch as crowding determines the visual discriminability of objects. Thus experiments suggest that only factors determining initial index-attachment (what we have called "grabbing")

or that require selecting among competing responses are relevant to tracking (the former conclusion received direct support from studies reported in Pylyshyn and Annan 2006).

5. These are simplifications based on interpretations of experimental findings. As is often the case in experimental psychology there is room for disagreement (Cavanagh and Alvarez 2005; Scholl 2009; but see Pylyshyn 2009).

6. FINST is an acronym for "fingers of instantiation": FINSTs are mental representations that serve to *instantiate*, or assign a value to, a variable, particularly a variable that serves as an argument to a function or predicate. The term first appeared in Pylyshyn, Elcock, Marmor, and Sander 1978.

7. This claim is too strong in general since one cannot rule out the possibility that a predicate like Inside(x,L) might be evaluated even if not all the arguments are bound to (or instantiated by) unique individual objects. The variables could be linked to a "filter" function that yields an object under appropriate circumstances, in which case the value of the predicate may be known even if the particular individual is not bound to one of the arguments of the predicate. In some programming systems this may be represented as Inside($x,L), where the term $x indicates a filter function that may determine if an object satisfying the predicate exists even if it is not indexed at the time. An even stronger version of this filter option might be one in which the filter indicates that there is some object x that satisfies the predicate (we might think of this as an existentially quantified variable ∃(x) which asserts that there is an object x that makes Inside(x,L) true even though x is not bound to the object at the time). Whether these alternatives occur in vision is a larger question that is outside the scope of the present theory.

8. Direct evidence for this claim is provided by Kimchi (2000); Parks (1994); Sekuler and Palmer (1992).

9. There is more to determining which objects correspond than just proximity and timing. In fact, a wide range of configural properties also bear on how correspondence is established (see Pylyshyn 2003b for a more detailed discussion), but they involve only spatiotemporal factors.

10. See http://www.yale.edu/perception/Brian/refGuides/MOT.html for a selective bibliography of publications using MOT, maintained by Brian Scholl (as of August 2014 there were 137 papers from 37 different peer-reviewed journals and many dozens more presented at meetings of the Vision Sciences Society).

11. The very concept of attentional resource is problematic (Franconeri 2013). For one thing, it is a free parameter, which makes it too easy to fit a pattern of performance.

12. In any case, it appears that in MOT objects are tracked in scene, rather than retinal, coordinates (Liu et al. 2005).

13. This is frequently misunderstood, since in computers one speaks of locations (and location-based retrieval). But even though data are at some location(s) or other at each instant in time (frequently distributed throughout the computer memory and changing rapidly as control shifts from program to program in the course of task-sharing random access memory), it is not by computing this sort of "location" that the data are retrieved from memory. The pointers correspond to addresses, which, in turn, are more perspicuously thought of as names or demonstratives rather than locations (for more on this point, see Pylyshyn 2003b).

14. Such heuristics are almost never available to introspection and are frequently recondite and surprising, as we will see in the examples below. This should not be taken to suggest that a heuristic is learned or discovered and represented as such. It's just a natural constraint whose origins are unknown (although it is tempting to assign them a teleological explanation).

15. This is just a special case of the general principle that explanations that appeal to natural selection are invariably post hoc. For discussion, see Fodor and Piattelli-Palmarini 2010.

16. The concept of an object is, of course, from time to time a constituent of *thoughts* (mostly, we suppose, of relatively abstract and sophisticated thoughts). That is, however, entirely neutral whether the "object concept" is primitive. In particular, we are *not* suggesting that OBJECT can

be *defined* in terms of the concept TRACKABLE; or, indeed that it can be defined at all. This is one of the reasons why, according to Pylyshyn (2007), FINSTs are said to be "grabbed by" (rather than applied to) *things* rather than to objects. Nobody thinks *thing* is a term of art.

17. Notice that the motion of the *proximal stimulus*—the motion of objects projected close to the viewer, such as on a computer screen or the retina—is never actually continuous, even when it is seen as such. This shows that whatever detects motion must do so *before* the information is passed on to the index-tracking system. This is compatible with what is known about how motion is detected by receptor cells very early in the visual system. See, e.g., Koch and Ullman 1985 for possible models of motion encoding.

18. It remains controversial whether the human early visual system encodes shapes in a viewpoint-independent manner or encodes a series of viewpoint-dependent two-dimensional shapes called *aspects*, or both.

19. It is no accident that researchers working on the development of canonical shapes count themselves as modularists (Biederman 1995; Bowyer and Dyer 1990; Koenderink 1990b; Marr 1982).

20. There are those who prefer to refer to some of the processes within the module as "inferences." So long as these processes are barred from contacting general knowledge—as opposed to what we have called natural constraints involving geometrical and spatiotemporal-optical properties—we don't consider this a departure from the modular view of vision, as we have discussed elsewhere (Fodor 1983; Pylyshyn 1999). Some of us prefer to reserve the term "inference" for the classical well-studied processes of deduction or induction (including probabilistic inference) that are not in principle prohibited from accessing the entire cognitive memory.

There are clearly topics or habits that may result in the processing of some representations being longer (e.g., taking more steps) and more error prone than others. Also, processes that operate more like a table lookup than a logical inference may well occur within the visual module without jeopardizing the modular view. An example of the latter might be limited forms of representation (which do not have access to universal quantifiers or negation) that can be processed rapidly and without combinatorial explosion. Such representations, which have been studied by Levesque (1986), are good examples of inference-like processes that do not violate the encapsulation requirement because their databases can be restricted.

21. For present purposes, a context is 'transparent' if and only if substitutions of coreferring expressions preserve truth in that context. Contexts that aren't transparent are said to be 'opaque'. See chapter 2.

5   Reference beyond the Perceptual Circle

1. It bears emphasis that, although mental representations may be structured (e.g., geometrically) at the stages of visual perceptual processing that we've been discussing, and although they refer to distal objects, the mental processes that take place are nonetheless assumed to be encapsulated. In particular, the vocabulary available to refer to basic-level distal objects is exiguous compared to what is routinely available to express the contents of perceptual beliefs at large. Maybe the former includes: ROUND, TRIANGULAR, ABOVE, BELOW, BLUE, FRONT, BACK, NEARER TO, FURTHER FROM, and other concepts that occur in typical basic-level representations; but it's assumed not to include: JOHN, JOHN'S TROUSERS, THE HOUSE NEXT DOOR, etc., even though all of those express properties that *non*basic objects can be perceived to have. Trousers are, perhaps, basic-level objects, in which case the concept TROUSERS may appear in the form-to-basic-category dictionary. But 'John's trousers' surely isn't a basic-level description (it's a mark of basic-level predicates that they are typically morphologically simple). Accordingly, John's trousers are seen as such only if they are seen as trousers, but not vice versa.

2. It used to be widely held (by pragmatists, verificationists, operationalists, procedural semanticists, and the like) that the distinction between "observable" and "theoretical" entities is central not only in epistemology but also in ontology and in theories of conceptual content, hence that ('strictly speaking') to say that the invention of the microscope made it possible to see paramecia is to equivocate either on 'paramecia'

or on 'see' (or both). This kind of thesis strikes us as a reductio of the ontology and semantics that led to it and has now gone largely out of fashion (however, see the appendix to chapter 2).

3. Sensations—pains, afterimages, ringings in your ears, and the like— are counterexamples, assuming that feeling an itch, hearing a ringing in your ears, and the like counts as perceiving it. Sensations are thus like percepts in some respects but not in others, and we don't understand why that's so. Many philosophers and psychologists have tried to explain it; but none of them has succeeded to the best of our knowledge. Dire epistemological issues turn on this, since it's often said that sensations are the sorts of mental things that their owners can't be mistaken about when they say or think that they are having them. We're neutral, however; we don't do epistemology.

4. It's not clear to us why merely counterfactual interpreters mightn't do for our purposes, since it is presumably not the case that actual interpreters serve as links in the causal chains that connect referents to perceivers that they interpret. But never mind.

5. It could be, however, that the complexity of SQUARE CIRCLE is, as one says, "merely implicit": that it appears only when the compositional structure of the concept is unpacked, i.e., at what linguists often (misleadingly) call "the semantic level," i.e., at the level of logical syntax.

6. The note of caution is because this sort of argument turns on some very uncertain assumptions about the modal behavior of proper names—in particular that they are "rigid designators"; and also because there isn't, in fact, any more of a story about the individuation of "conceptual roles" than there is about the individuation of meanings (see chapter 2). Indeed, the familiar dilemma about holism versus analyticity arises in the former just as it is in the latter. How different must the stories be for 'The Lone Ranger' to refer in one but not the other?

7. Naturalists who like IRS often take for granted that the *inferential* role of a concept can be explicated as something like *its causal role in mental processes*. (See, e.g., Block 1978.) But it's hard to see how this could work unless the distinction between "mental" processes and others assumes that the former are themselves ipso facto intensional, in which case the

familiar circularities reappear. This is a special case of a point we will presently emphasize: prima facie, 'dog' and 'cat' are different in inferential role; 'that's a dog' implies 'that's a canine' but 'that's a cat' implies 'that's a feline'. But this constitutes a difference in inferential role only on the assumption that 'canine' and 'feline' *aren't synonyms*. We strongly suspect that inferential role semanticists who claim to be naturalistic are doomed to running in this sort of circle.

8. For example, it can't be *semantically necessary* that Iago was a stinker; he might have been quite a good fellow if his childhood had been happier.

9. "What about things that are too small for anyone *ever* to perceive them—protons, for example?" Well, adding appropriate links to causal chains has made it possible to *detect* protons. Does seeing a proton's trace on a photographic plate count as seeing a proton? Or does it count as only seeing a trace of a proton? If you think that deep issues in epistemology (or in ontology, or in semantics) turn on this (as philosophers did who cared a lot about the distinction between "observations" and "theoretical inferences"), you are free to adjust the boundaries of the PC to suit your philosophical commitments. All that matters, according to our understanding of what content is, is that though such adjustments may affect what one says about seeing, they needn't affect what one says about referring. We think that is itself an argument for understanding content in the way we've been urging you to do.

10. It doesn't, of course, follow from PRS that some, all, or even any of one's concepts actually *are* learned; it doesn't even follow that there *is* such a thing as learning. All those are left as empirical issues (as they should be; ethology is not an a priori science, legions of philosophers to the contrary notwithstanding).

11. The notion of a law of nature is, of course, intensional, and there are laws of physics (chemistry, mechanics, etc.) that apply to chairs, but, on our view, none of those apply to chairs *as such*. But it would be a mistake to argue, by analogy, that there are no *psychological* laws about chairs. To the contrary, it seems entirely plausible that if a chair is in one's perceptual circle (and if the appropriate background conditions

are satisfied) then it is *nomologically necessary* that it would cause certain mental things to happen (in particular that it would cause certain mental representations to be tokened in minds like ours). It might, for example, be nomologically necessary that if a chair were now in your perceptual circle, it would now cause a token of a Mentalese representation that is coreferential with the word 'chair' to be tokened. That sounds OK to us.

12. The idea that some (or even all) concepts are individuated by their possession conditions is, of course, by no means novel; see, e.g., Sellars 1963; and something of the sort may well be implicit in Wittgenstein. But that kind of semantics is generally suggested as a general *alternative* to referential semantics, thus assimilating the semantics of bona fide referential concepts (TREE, CICERO) to "logical" concepts like AND (and, in our view, making the question of how concepts can have extensions appear insoluble [Brandom 2000]). Inferences from 'Some xs are F' to 'All xs are F' should be avoided whenever possible.

References

Alvarez, G. A., and S. L. Franconeri. 2007. How many objects can you attentively track? Evidence for a resource-limited tracking mechanism. *Journal of Vision* 7 (13): 1–10.

Armstrong, S., L. Gleitman, and H. Gleitman. 1983. What some concepts might not be. *Cognition* 13:263–308.

Arriagada, J., P. Olausson, and A. Selimovic. 2002. Artificial neural network simulator for SOFC performance prediction. *Journal of Power Sources* 112 (1): 54–60.

Berkeley, G. [1709] 2007. *An Essay Towards a New Theory of Vision.* Ann Arbor: University of Michigan Press.

Biederman, I. 1987. Recognition-by-components: A theory of human image interpretation. *Psychological Review* 94:115–148.

Biederman, I. 1995. Visual object recognition. In *Visual Cognition*, 2nd ed., ed. S. M. Kosslyn and D. N. Osherson. Cambridge, MA: MIT Press.

Block, N. J. 1978. Troubles with functionalism. In *Perception and Cognition: Issues in the Foundations of Psychology*, vol. 9, ed. C. W. Savage. Minneapolis: University of Minnesota Press.

Bowyer, K. W., and C. R. Dyer. 1990. Aspect graphs: An introduction and survey of recent results. *International Journal of Imaging Systems and Technology* 2 (4): 315–328.

Brandom, R. 2000. *Articulating Reasons*. Cambridge, MA: Harvard University Press.

Brown, C. M. 1984. Computer vision and natural constraints. *Science* 224 (4655): 1299–1305.

Bruner, J. S., J. J. Goodnow, and G. A. Austin. [1956] 1986. *A Study of Thinking*. New Brunswick, NJ: Transaction Books.

Carnap, R. 1956. *Meaning and Necessity: A Study in Semantics and Modal Logic*. Chicago: University of Chicago Press.

Cavanagh, P., and G. A. Alvarez. 2005. Tracking multiple targets with multifocal attention. *Trends in Cognitive Sciences* 9 (7): 349–354.

Chomsky, N. 1959. A review of B. F. Skinner's *Verbal Behavior*. *Language* 35 (1): 26–58.

Chomsky, N. 2003. Reply to Poland. In *Chomsky and His Critics*, ed. L. Antony and N. Hornstein. Oxford: Blackwell.

Churchland, P. M. 1980. Plasticity: Conceptual and neuronal. *Behavioral and Brain Sciences* 3:133–134.

Churchland, P. M. 2006. Relevant abduction, vector completion, and the capacity for "global sensitive" inferences. In *Cognitive Penetrability and the Problem of Induction*, ed. A. Raftopoulus. New York: Nova Publishers.

Churchland, P. M., and P. S. Churchland. 1983. Stalking the wild epistemic engine. *Noûs* 17:5–18.

Clark, A. 2000. *A Theory of Sentience*. New York: Oxford University Press.

Davidson, D. 1970. Mental events. In *Experience and Theory*, ed. L. Foster and J. Swanson. London: Duckworth.

Dawson, M., and Z. W. Pylyshyn. 1988. Natural constraints in apparent motion. In *Computational Processes in Human Vision: An Interdisciplinary Perspective*, ed. Z. W. Pylyshyn, 99–120. Stamford, CT: Ablex Publishing.

Dennett, D. C. 1991. *Consciousness Explained*. Boston: Little, Brown.

Dennis, J. L., and Z. W. Pylyshyn. 2002. Effect of object discriminability on multiple object tracking. *Journal of Vision* 2 (7): 241.

Devitt, M. 2006. *Ignorance of Language*. Oxford: Oxford University Press.

Feldman, J. A., and D. H. Ballard. 1982. Connectionist models and their properties. *Cognitive Science* 6:205–254.

Fodor, J. A. 1975. *The Language of Thought*. New York: Crowell.

Fodor, J. A. 1978. Tom Swift and his procedural grandmother. *Cognition* 6:229–247.

Fodor, J. A. 1983. *The Modularity of Mind: An Essay on Faculty Psychology*. Cambridge, MA: MIT Press.

Fodor, J. A. 1998. *Concepts: Where Cognitive Science Went Wrong*. Oxford: Oxford University Press.

Fodor, J. A. 2000. *The Mind Doesn't Work That Way: The Scope and Limits of Computational Psychology*. Cambridge, MA: MIT Press.

Fodor, J. A. 2001. Language, thought, and compositionality. *Mind and Language* 16 (1): 1–15.

Fodor, J. A. 2004. Having concepts: A brief refutation of the twentieth century. *Mind and Language* 19 (1): 29–47.

Fodor, J. A. 2009. Enough with the norms, already. In *Reduction: Between the Mind and the Brain*, ed. A. Hieke and H. Leitgeb. Frankfurt: Ontos Verlag.

Fodor, J. A. 2010. *LOT 2: The Language of Thought Revisited*. Oxford: Oxford University Press.

Fodor, J. A., T. Bever, and M. Garrett. 1974. *The Psychology of Language*. New York: McGraw-Hill.

Fodor, J. A., and E. Lepore. 1992. *Holism: A Shopper's Guide*. London: Blackwell.

Fodor, J. A., and M. Piattelli-Palmarini. 2010. *What Darwin Got Wrong*. New York: Farrar, Straus & Giroux.

Fodor, J. A., and Z. W. Pylyshyn. 1981. How direct is visual perception? Some reflections on Gibson's "ecological approach." *Cognition* 9:139–196.

Fodor, J. A., and Z. W. Pylyshyn. 1988. Connectionism and cognitive architecture: A critical analysis. *Cognition* 28:3–71.

Franconeri, S. L. 2013. The nature and status of visual resources. In *Oxford Handbook of Cognitive Psychology*, ed. D. Reisberg. Oxford: Oxford University Press.

Franconeri, S. L., S. J. Jonathan, and J. M. Scimeca. 2010. Tracking multiple objects is limited only by object spacing, not by speed, time, or capacity. *Psychological Science* 21:920–925.

Franconeri, S. L., J. Lin, Z. Pylyshyn, B. Fisher, and J. Enns. 2008. Evidence against a speed limit in multiple-object tracking. *Psychonomic Bulletin and Review* 15 (4): 802–808.

Franconeri, S. L., Z. W. Pylyshyn, and B. J. Scholl. 2012. A simple proximity heuristic allows tracking of multiple objects through occlusion. *Attention, Perception, and Psychophysics* 72 (4): 691–702.

Gleitman, L., and A. Papafragou. 2005. Language and thought. In *The Cambridge Handbook of Thinking and Reasoning*, ed. K. J. Holyoak and R. G. Morrison, 633–661. New York: Cambridge University Press.

Gogel, W. C. [1973] 1997. The organization of perceived space. In *Indirect Perception*, ed. I. Rock, 361–386. Cambridge, MA: MIT Press.

Green, C., and D. Bavelier. 2006. Enumeration versus multiple object tracking: The case of action video game players. *Cognition* 101 (1): 217–245.

Hoffman, D. D. 1998. *Visual Intelligence: How We Create What We See.* New York: W. W. Norton.

Humphreys, G. W., and M. J. Riddoch. 1987. *To See But Not to See: A Case Study of Visual Agnosia.* Hillsdale, NJ: Erlbaum.

Jackson, E. 1977. *Perception.* Cambridge: Cambridge University Press.

Johnson, M. 1995. Memoization of top-down parsing. *Computational Linguistics* 21 (93): 405–417.

Jolicoeur, P. 1999. Concurrent response-selection demands modulate the attentional blink. *Journal of Experimental Psychology: Human Perception and Performance* 25 (4): 1097–1113.

Kahneman, D., A. Treisman, and B. J. Gibbs. 1992. The reviewing of object files: Object-specific integration of information. *Cognitive Psychology* 24 (2): 175–219.

Kanwisher, N. 1991. Repetition blindness and illusory conjunctions: Errors in binding visual types with visual tokens. *Journal of Experimental Psychology: Human Perception and Performance* 17 (2): 404–421.

Keane, B. P., and Z. W. Pylyshyn. 2006. Is motion extrapolation employed in multiple object tracking? Tracking as a low-level, non-predictive function. *Cognitive Psychology* 52 (4): 346–368.

Kimchi, R. 2000. The perceptual organization of visual objects: A microgenetic analysis. *Vision Research* 40 (10–12): 1333–1347.

Koch, C., and S. Ullman. 1985. Shifts in selective visual attention: Towards the underlying neural circuitry. *Human Neurobiology* 4: 219–227.

Koenderink, J. J. 1990a. The brain a geometry engine. *Psychological Research* 52 (2–3): 122–127.

Koenderink, J. J. 1990b. *Solid Shape*. Cambridge, MA: MIT Press.

Kolers, P. A., and M. Von Grunau. 1976. Shape and colour in apparent motion. *Vision Research* 16:329–335.

Kosslyn, S. M. 1975. The information represented in visual images. *Cognitive Psychology* 7:341–370.

Kosslyn, S. M. 1994. *Image and Brain: The Resolution of the Imagery Debate*. Cambridge, MA: MIT Press.

Kripke, S. 1980. *Naming and Necessity*. Cambridge, MA: Harvard University Press.

Kripke, S. 1982. *Wittgenstein on Rules and Private Language*. Cambridge, MA: Harvard University Press.

Leonard, C. J., and Z. W. Pylyshyn. 2003. Measuring the attention demand of multiple object tracking (MOT) [Abstract of poster presentation at VSS 2003]. *Journal of Vision* 3.

Leslie, A. M. 1988. The necessity of illusion: Perception and thought in infancy. In *Thought without Language*, ed. L. Weiskrantz. Oxford: Oxford Science Publications.

Levesque, H. 1986. Making believers out of computers. *Artificial Intelligence* 30:81–108.

Levesque, H., and R. J. Brachman. 1985. A fundamental tradeoff in knowledge representation and reasoning (revised version). In *Readings in Knowledge Representation*, ed. H. J. Levesque and R. J. Brachman, 41–70. Los Altos, CA: Morgan Kaufmann.

Li, P., L. Abarnell, L. Gleitman, and A. Papafragou. 2011. Spatial reasoning in Tenejapan Mayans. *Cognition* 120:33–53.

Lindberg, D. C. 1976. *Theories of Vision from al-Kindi to Kepler*. Chicago: University of Chicago Press.

Liu, G., E. L. Austen, K. S. Booth, B. D. Fisher, R. Argue, M. I. Rempel, et al. 2005. Multiple-object tracking is based on scene, not retinal, coordinates. *Journal of Experimental Psychology: Human Perception and Performance* 31 (2): 235–247.

Mandler, G., and B. Shebo. 1982. Subitizing: An analysis of its component processes. *Journal of Experimental Psychology: General* 111:1–22.

Marr, D. 1982. *Vision: A Computational Investigation into the Human Representation and Processing of Visual Information*. San Francisco: W. H. Freeman.

Marr, D., and H. K. Nishihara. 1978. Representation and recognition of the spatial organization of three-dimensional shapes. *Proceedings of the Royal Society of London, Series B: Biological Sciences* 200:269–294.

Mervis, C. B., and E. Rosch. 1981. Categorization of natural objects. *Annual Review of Psychology* 32:89–115.

Michie, D. 1968. Memo functions and machine learning. *Nature* 218:19–22.

Milner, A. D., and M. A. Goodale. 1995. *The Visual Brain in Action*. New York: Oxford University Press.

O'Regan, J. K. 1992. Solving the "real" mysteries of visual perception: The world as an outside memory. *Canadian Journal of Psychology* 46:461–488.

O'Regan, J. K., and A. Noë. 2002. A sensorimotor account of vision and visual consciousness. *Behavioral and Brain Sciences* 24 (5): 939–1031.

Paivio, A. 1971. *Imagery and Verbal Processes*. New York: Holt, Reinhart & Winston.

Paivio, A. 1977. Images, propositions, and knowledge. In *Images, Perception, and Knowledge*, ed. J. M. Nicholas. Dordrech: Reidel.

Paivio, A. 1991. Dual coding theory: Retrospect and current status. *Canadian Journal of Psychology* 45 (3): 255–287.

Parks, T. E. 1994. On the microgenesis of illusory figures: A failure to replicate. *Perception* 23:857–862.

Pentland, A. 1987. Recognition by parts. Paper presented at the International Conference on Computer Vision.

Prinz, J., and A. Clark. 2004. Putting concepts to work: Some thoughts for the twenty-first century. *Mind and Language* 19 (1): 57–69.

Putnam, H. 2012. *Philosophy in an Age of Science*. Cambridge, MA: Harvard University Press.

Pylyshyn, Z. W. 1973. What the mind's eye tells the mind's brain: A critique of mental imagery. *Psychological Bulletin* 80:1–24.

Pylyshyn, Z. W. 1981. The imagery debate: Analogue media versus tacit knowledge. *Psychological Review* 88:16–45.

Pylyshyn, Z. W. 1989. The role of location indexes in spatial perception: A sketch of the FINST spatial-index model. *Cognition* 32:65–97.

Pylyshyn, Z. W. 1999. Is vision continuous with cognition? The case for cognitive impenetrability of visual perception. *Behavioral and Brain Sciences* 22 (3): 341–423.

Pylyshyn, Z. W. 2001. Visual indexes, preconceptual objects, and situated vision. *Cognition* 80 (1/2): 127–158.

Pylyshyn, Z. W. 2002. Mental imagery: In search of a theory. *Behavioral and Brain Sciences* 25 (2): 157–237.

Pylyshyn, Z. W. 2003a. Return of the mental image: Are there really pictures in the brain? *Trends in Cognitive Sciences* 7 (3): 113–118.

Pylyshyn, Z. W. 2003b. *Seeing and Visualizing: It's Not What You Think.* Cambridge, MA: MIT Press.

Pylyshyn, Z. W. 2007. *Things and Places: How the Mind Connects with the World.* Jean Nicod Lecture Series. Cambridge, MA: MIT Press.

Pylyshyn, Z. W. 2009. Perception, representation, and the world: The FINST that binds. In *Computation, Cognition, and Pylyshyn*, ed. D. Dedrick and L. M. Trick. Cambridge, MA: MIT Press.

Pylyshyn, Z. W., and V. Annan, Jr. 2006. Dynamics of target selection in multiple object tracking (MOT). *Spatial Vision* 19 (6): 485–504.

Pylyshyn, Z. W., E. W. Elcock, M. Marmor, and P. Sander. 1978. Explorations in visual-motor spaces. Paper presented at the Second International Conference of the Canadian Society for Computational Studies of Intelligence, University of Toronto.

Quine, W. V. O. 1951. Two dogmas of empiricism. *Philosophical Review* 60:20–43.

Quine, W. V. O. 1960. *Word and Object.* Cambridge, MA: MIT Press.

Quine, W. V. O. 1981. The nature of natural knowledge [1975]. In *Mind and Language*, ed. S. Guttenplan, 67–81. Oxford: Oxford University Press.

Richards, W. 1980. Natural computation: Filing a perceptual void. Paper presented at the Tenth Annual Conference on Modelling and Simulation, University of Pittsburgh.

Richards, W., ed. 1988. *Natural Computation*. Cambridge, MA: MIT Press.

Rock, I. 1983. *The Logic of Perception*. Cambridge, MA: MIT Press.

Rosch, E. H., C. B. Mervis, W. D. Gray, D. M. Johnson, and P. Boyes-Braem. 1976. Basic objects in natural categories. *Cognitive Psychology* 8:382–439.

Ryle, G. 1949. *The Concept of Mind*. London: Hutchinson.

Sartre, J.-P. 1948. *The Psychology of Imagination*. New York: Philosophical Library.

Scholl, B. J. 2009. What have we learned about attention from multiple-object tracking (and vice versa)? In *Computation, Cognition, and Pylyshyn*, ed. D. Dedrick and L. Trick, 49–78. Cambridge, MA: MIT Press.

Scholl, B. J., and Z. W. Pylyshyn. 1999. Tracking multiple items through occlusion: Clues to visual objecthood. *Cognitive Psychology* 38 (2): 259–290.

Scholl, B. J., Z. W. Pylyshyn, and J. Feldman. 2001. What is a visual object: Evidence from target-merging in multiple-object tracking. *Cognition* 80:159–177.

Scholl, B. J., Z. W. Pylyshyn, and S. L. Franconeri. 1999a. The relationship between property-encoding and object-based attention: Evidence from multiple-object tracking. Unpublished manuscript.

Scholl, B. J., Z. W. Pylyshyn, and S. L. Franconeri. 1999b. When are featural and spatiotemporal properties encoded as a result of attentional allocation? *Investigative Ophthalmology and Visual Science* 40 (4): 4195.

Sekuler, A. B., and S. E. Palmer. 1992. Visual completion of partly occluded objects: A microgenetic analysis. *Journal of Experimental Psychology: General* 121:95–111.

Sellars, W. 1963. *Science, Perception, and Reality*. New York: The Humanities Press. (Reissued in 1991 by Ridgeview Publishing, Atascadero, CA.)

Shepard, R. N. 1964. Attention and the metrical structure of the similarity space. *Journal of Mathematical Psychology* 1:54–87.

Skinner, B. F. [1957] 1992. *Verbal Behavior*. Acton, MA: Copley Publishing.

Soames, S. 2010. *Philosophy of Language*. Princeton: Princeton University Press.

Spelke, E. S. 1990. Principles of object perception. *Cognitive Science* 14:29–56.

Sperling, G. 1967. Successive approximations to a model for short term memory. *Acta Psychologica* 27:285–292.

Sperling, G., and E. Weichselgartner. 1995. Episodic theory of the dynamics of spatial attention. *Psychological Review* 102 (3): 503–532.

Strawson, P. F. 1959. *Individuals: An Essay in Descriptive Metaphysics*. London: Methuen.

Treisman, A. 1988. Features and objects: The Fourteenth Bartlett Memorial Lecture. *Quarterly Journal of Experimental Psychology* 40A (2): 201–237.

Trick, L. M., F. Jaspers-Fayer, and N. Sethi. 2005. Multiple-object tracking in children: The "Catch the Spies" task. *Cognitive Development* 20 (3): 373–387.

Trick, L. M., and Z. W. Pylyshyn. 1994. Why are small and large numbers enumerated differently? A limited capacity preattentive stage in vision. *Psychological Review* 101 (1): 80–102.

Ullman, S. 1979. *The Interpretation of Visual Motion*. Cambridge, MA: MIT Press.

Ullman, S. 1984. Visual routines. *Cognition* 18:97–159.

Watson, D. G., and G. W. Humphreys. 1999. The magic number four and temporo-parietal damage: Neurological impairments in counting targets amongst distractors. *Cognitive Neuropsychology* 16 (7): 609–629.

Wender, K. F., and R. Rothkegel. 2000. Subitizing and its subprocesses. *Psychological Research* 64 (2): 81–92.

Wilson, E. O. 2013. *Letters to a Young Scientist.* New York: W. W. Norton.

Wittgenstein, Ludwig. 1958. *Philosophical Investigations*, 2nd ed. Trans. G. E. M. Anscombe. Oxford: Blackwell.

Wittgenstein, Ludwig. 1979. *Wittgenstein's Lectures, 1932–35.* Ed. Alice Ambrose. London: Blackwell.

Index